Selected and edited by
Andrew and Janet Goodwyn

Oxford University Press

Oxford University Press, Walton Street, Oxford OX2 6DP

Oxford New York Toronto
Delhi Bombay Calcutta Madras Karachi
Kuala Lumpur Singapore Hong Kong Tokyo
Nairobi Dar es Salaam Cape Town
Melbourne Auckland Madrid

and associated companies in
Berlin Ibadan

Oxford is a trade mark of Oxford University Press

© Selection and activities: Andrew and Janet Goodwyn

ISBN 0 19 831279 2

All rights reserved. No part of this publication may be reproduced, stored in a retrieval system, or transmitted, in any form or by any means, without the prior permission in writing of Oxford University Press. Within the UK, exceptions are allowed in respect of any fair dealing for the purpose of research or private study, or criticism or review, as permitted under the Copyright, Designs and Patents Act, 1988 or in the case of reprographic reproduction in accordance with the terms of licenses issued by the Copyright Licensing Agency. Enquiries concerning reproduction outside those terms and in other countries should be sent to the Rights Department, Oxford University Press, at the address above.

Typeset by Pentacor *PLC*, High Wycombe, Bucks
Printed and bound in Great Britain by
Butler & Tanner Ltd, Frome and London

Cover illustration by Mark Oldroyd

Also available in the *Oxford Literature Resources* series:

Contemporary Stories 1	0 19 831251 2
Contemporary Stories 2	0 19 831254 7
Stories from South Asia	0 19 831255 5
Science Fiction Stories	0 19 831261 X
Fantasy Stories	0 19 831262 8
Sport	0 19 831264 4
Autobiography	0 19 831265 2
Crime Stories	0 19 831280 6
Scottish Short Stories	0 19 831281 4
American Short Stories	0 19 831282 2
Travel Writing	0 19 831283 0

Contents

Acknowledgements	v
Preface	vii
Romantic Love	1
Love *Grace Nichols*	1
Love *Philip Larkin*	2
Love *Atkinson, Atkinson, and Hilgard*	3
Love on the Bon-Dieu *Kate Chopin*	6
By Grand Central Station I Sat Down and Wept *Elizabeth Smart*	18
The Song of Solomon *The Bible*	23
Right from the Heart *Stephen Burgen*	25
The End of Something *Ernest Hemingway*	27
Jealous Love	32
Roman Fever *Edith Wharton* (*adapted for radio by Janet Goodwyn*)	32
The Demon Lover *Elizabeth Bowen*	49
An Attempt at Jealousy *Craig Raine*	57
Song: Go, and Catch a Falling Star *John Donne*	59
Loving the Family and Other Animals	60
A Domestic Dilemma *Carson McCullers*	60
Arrangements *Douglas Dunn*	71
An Arundel Tomb *Philip Larkin*	73
Romeo and Juliet (from Act III Scene 5) *William Shakespeare*	75
Brothers and Sisters *Alice Walker*	80
Father to Son *Elizabeth Jennings*	85
Long Distance *Tony Harrison*	86
Flight *Doris Lessing*	88
Death of an Old Dog *Antonia Fraser*	94
The Lady Who Loved Insects *Anon* (*translated by Arthur Waley*)	105

Contents

Comradely Love — 112

A Sight in Camp in the Daybreak Grey and Dim
Walt Whitman — 112
Greater Love *Wilfred Owen* — 113
On Jane Austen's Death *Cassandra Austen* — 114
The Girl in the Pink Hat *Charlotte Perkins Gilman* — 117
Tich Miller *Wendy Cope* — 125
Daphne Morse *Pamela Gillilan* — 126

Activities — 127

Extended Activities — 144

Wider Reading — 147

Acknowledgements

The editor and publisher are grateful for permission to include the following copyright material in this collection:

R. L. Atkinson, R. C. Atkinson & E. R. Hilgard, 'Love' from *Introduction to Psychology* (Harcourt, Brace Jovanovich 1981). **Elizabeth Bowen**, 'The Demon Lover' from *The Collected Stories of Elizabeth Bowen*. Reprinted by permission of Random House UK Ltd on behalf of the Estate of the author, and Jonathan Cape as publisher. **Stephen Burgen**, 'Right from the heart', from *The Guardian*, February 8, 1992. © The Guardian 1992 and used with permission. **Wendy Cope** 'Tich Miller' from *Making Cocoa for Kingsley Amis*. Reprinted by permission of Faber & Faber Ltd. **Douglas Dunn**, 'Arrangements' from *Elegies*. Reprinted by permission of Faber & Faber Ltd. **Antonia Fraser**: 'Death of an Old Dog' from *The Mammoth Book of Modern Crime Stories*, ed. George Hardinge. © Antonia Fraser. **Pamela Gillilan**, 'Daphne Morse'. Reprinted by permission of the author. **Elizabeth Jennings**: 'Father to Son' from *Collected Poems* (Carcanet Press). Reprinted by permission of David Higham Associates Ltd. **Philip Larkin**: 'Love' and 'An Arundel Tomb' from *Collected Poems*. Reprinted by permission of Faber & Faber Ltd. **Doris Lessing**, 'Flight' from *The Habit of Loving* (MacGibbon & Kee, 1957). **Carson McCullers**, 'A Domestic Dilemma' from *The Ballad of the Sad Café*. Copyright Carson McCullers 1951. **Grace Nichols**, 'Love' from *Lazy Thoughts of a Lazy Woman* (Virago, 1989). **Craig Raine**, 'An Attempt at Jealousy' from *Rich*. Reprinted by permission of Faber & Faber Ltd. **Elizabeth Smart**, extract from *By Grand Central Station I Sat Down and Wept* (Paladin/Grafton Books, 1991). **Alice Walker**, 'Brothers and Sisters' from *In Search of Our Mothers' Gardens*, published by The Women's Press Ltd, 1984. Reprinted by permission of David Higham Associates Ltd.

Every effort has been made to secure reprint permission from

Acknowledgements

copyright holders prior to publication. However, in some instances this has not proved successful. If contacted the publisher will be pleased to rectify any errors or omissions at the earliest opportunity.

Preface

There must be more views of what love is than of any other facet of human life. Equally there are millions of references to love in all its forms in every aspect of literature. On any given day the media will be full of who is in love or out of love with whom and of the myriad things that have happened as a result of the most extraordinary of all human emotions.

In this collection we have tried to encompass what we feel are some of the most important aspects of love, aspects which affect us in our daily lives. So we begin with romantic love as most people think of this side of love before all others. For many finding the love of their life, a 'true love', is the most important purpose in life itself. It is so vital that love very easily turns to hate. Can there be love without jealousy? We felt it important to explore the darker side to the passions experienced by all.

But although romantic love dominates some people's lives, we all have competing and complementary loves going on at the same time. In all cultures the family is an extraordinary source of intense emotions; family love is linked to romantic love, but it is certainly not the same kind of love.

And what of love of friends? Some people have many friends, some a few, some may have none. There is no doubt however that there is a deep human need for friendship, for companionship and for comradeship. Comradeship is hard to define but often arises in very particular circumstances, for example in wartime. For many people feelings of affection extend to the animal world. There are plenty of jokes about the way people's pets end up looking like their owners but, more seriously, we know that there can be a genuine bond between people and animals that could only be described as love.

For some people love of an idea or a religion or a place can be as powerful as any human love. Indeed some argue that these forms of love and particularly love of country and love of God are really the highest forms that we can aspire to. One result is

Preface

that history is full of stories about those who died to keep some kind of faith.

Throughout the collection you will find writers dealing with complex patterns of love, often where divergent kinds of love cause intense conflicts in society or for the individual. In this way love can be deadly serious, yet for much of the time it is not only our mainspring of happiness but also a rich source of humour; love makes us cry and laugh.

The collection includes a wide range of texts, poems, stories, a radio play, extract from novels and plays and also different types of non-fiction. Writers from around the English speaking world are represented and through reading their work readers will discover that although we are all different in culture or as individuals, yet we have much in common when it comes to love. The follow-on activities encourage readers to question assumptions about love and writers' attitudes to it. The 'language of love' is also considered and there are opportunities for a wide range of written and discussion work to satisfy many of the requirements for GCSE and Standard Grade. The collection, we hope, provides something for everyone and offers a broad reading experience in a boundless subject.

Andrew and Janet Goodwyn

Romantic Love
Love

Grace Nichols

Love is not a grindstone
constantly grinding
wearing down to bone

Love is not an interlocking
deadlock
of inseparable flesh
or a merging of metals
to smooth alloy

Love is a sunshawl
that keeps the beloved warm

Even the undeserving
love floods
risking all.

Love

Philip Larkin

The difficult part of love
Is being selfish enough,
Is having the blind persistence
To upset an existence
Just for your own sake.
what cheek it must take.

And then the unselfish side –
How can you be satisfied,
Putting someone else first
So that you come off worst?
My life is for me.
As well ignore gravity.

Still, vicious or virtuous,
Love suits most of us.
Only the bleeder found
Selfish this wrong way round
Is ever wholly rebuffed,
And he can get stuffed.

Love

Atkinson, Atkinson and Hilgard

The process by which relationships move from liking towards closeness and intimacy has been called *social penetration* (Altman and Taylor, 1973). Social penetration has both breadth and depth. Breadth refers to the number of different areas of the partners' lives and personalities that are involved in the relationship, and depth refers to the degree to which the pair know and share things that are close to the cores of their personalities – fears, anxieties, uncertainties, hopes, and so forth.

The key to social penetration is reciprocal self-disclosure; the partners must gradually reveal themselves to each other, and this can be a very delicate process. At the beginning of a relationship, there is a strong *norm of reciprocity*; as one person begins to disclose things about himself or herself, the other person must also be willing to do so. In this way, trust builds and intimacy increases. Research shows that the pace of self-disclosure is very important. If one of the partners discloses too much too soon, it can cause the other person to pull back (Rubin, 1975).

In romantic relationships these days, self-disclosure takes place rather early. In one recent study, most of the couples who had been going together an average of eight months had engaged in full and equal disclosure about very personal and private areas of their lives (Rubin and others, 1980). About three fourths of the women and men said they had fully revealed their feelings about their sexual relationship; almost half had fully disclosed their thoughts about the future of the relationship; and over half had provided full information about their previous sexual experiences. A third of each sex had revealed fully those things about themselves that they were most ashamed of.

Such rapid and full self-disclosure has not always been the norm. In one study, both college students and senior citizens were asked to describe relationships characteristic of 22-year-olds of their own generations. It was found that today's young people expect pairs to disclose both positive and negative feelings more openly and freely than previous generations (Rands and Levinger, 1979). Up through the 1950s, the middle-class norm emphasized much more self-restraint and self-protectiveness. The sexual revolution of the 1960s changed not only sexual behaviour but also social norms concerning self-disclosure (Altman and Taylor, 1973). This was the era of the encounter group and instant intimacy. Although much of the popularity of encounter groups has declined, the new norms of self-disclosure have been sustained in romantic relationships.

The concept of romantic love is an old one, but the belief that it has much to do with marriage is more recent and far from universal. In some non-Western cultures, marriage is still considered to be a contractual or financial arrangement that has nothing whatever to do with love. In our own society, the link between love and marriage has actually become stronger in the past 15 years. In 1967, about two thirds of college men but only about one fourth of college women stated that they would not marry a person they did not love even if the person had all the other qualities they desired (Kephart, 1967). Perhaps the women at that time had to be more practical about their financial security. But in a 1976 replication of the study, it was found that a full 86 percent of men and 80 percent of the women would now refuse to marry without being in love. In fact, these researchers report that many young men and women believe that if romantic love disappears from the relationship, that is sufficient reason to end it (Campbell and Berscheid, 1976).

A study of long-term marriages in the United States and Japan suggests that these romantic views may change with time. The American marriages started out with a higher level of love than did the Japanese arranged marriages, as measured by expressions of affection, sexual interest, and marital satisfaction. Love decreased in both groups, and after 10 years, there were no differences (Blood, 1967). As the sixteenth-century writer

Giraldi put it: 'The history of a love affair is in some sense the drama of its fight against time.'

This does not imply, however, that all the marriages were failures: some couples had gratifying marriages, and others experienced failure. The successful marriages were characterized by communication between the partners, an equitable division of labour, and equality of decision-making power. Romantic love is terrific for starters, but the sustaining forces of a good long-term relationship are less exciting, undoubtedly require more work, and have more to do with equality than with passion. A disappointment for romantics, perhaps, but heartening news and powerful propaganda for advocates of sexual equality.

Love on the Bon-Dieu

Kate Chopin

Upon a pleasant veranda of Père Antoine's cottage, that adjoined the church, a young girl had long been seated, awaiting his return. It was the eve of Easter Sunday, and since early afternoon the priest had been engaged in hearing the confessions of those who wished to make their Easters the following day. The girl did not seem impatient at his delay; on the contrary, it was very restful to her to lie back in the big chair she had found there, and peep through the thick curtain of vines at the people who occasionally passed along the village street.

She was slender, with a frailness that indicated lack of wholesome and plentiful nourishment. A pathetic, uneasy look was in her grey eyes, and even faintly stamped her features, which were fine and delicate. In lieu of a hat, a barège veil covered her light brown and abundant hair. She wore a coarse white cotton 'josie', and a blue calico skirt that only half concealed her tattered shoes.

As she sat there, she held carefully in her lap a parcel of eggs securely fastened in a red bandana handkerchief.

Twice already a handsome, stalwart young man in quest of the priest had entered the yard, and penetrated to where she sat. At first they had exchanged the uncompromising 'howdy' of strangers, and nothing more. The second time, finding the priest still absent, he hesitated to go at once. Instead, he stood upon the step, and narrowing his brown eyes, gazed beyond the river, off towards the west, where a murky streak of mist was spreading across the sun.

'It look like mo' rain,' he remarked, slowly and carelessly.

'We done had 'bout 'nough,' she replied, in much the same tone.

'It's no chance to thin out the cotton,' he went on.

'An' the Bon-Dieu,' she resumed, 'it's on'y today you can cross him on foot.'

'You live yonda on the Bon-Dieu, *donc?*' he asked, looking at her for the first time since he had spoken.

'Yas, by Nid d'Hibout, m'sieur.'

Instinctive courtesy held him from questioning her further. But he seated himself on the step, evidently determined to wait there for the priest. He said no more, but sat scanning critically the steps, the porch, and pillar beside him, from which he occasionally tore away little pieces of detached wood, where it was beginning to rot at its base.

A click at the side gate that communicated with the churchyard soon announced Père Antoine's return. He came hurriedly across the garden path, between the tall, lusty rosebushes that lined either side of it, which were now fragrant with blossoms. His long, flapping cassock added something of height to his undersized, middle-aged figure, as did the skullcap which rested securely back on his head. He saw only the young man at first, who rose at his approach.

'Well, Azenor,' he called cheerily in French, extending his hand. 'How is this? I expected you all the week.'

'Yes, monsieur; but I knew well what you wanted with me, and I was finishing the doors for Gros-Léon's new house;' saying which, he drew back, and indicated by a motion and look that some one was present who had a prior claim upon Père Antoine's attention.

'Ah, Lalie!' the priest exclaimed, when he had mounted the porch, and saw her there behind the vines. 'Have you been waiting here since you confessed? Surely an hour ago!'

'Yes, monsieur.'

'You should rather have made some visits in the village, child'

'I am not acquainted with any one in the village,' she returned.

The priest, as he spoke, had drawn a chair, and seated himself beside her, with his hands comfortably clasping his knees. He wanted to know how things were out on the bayou.

'And how is the grandmother?' he asked 'As cross and crabbed as ever? And with that' – he added reflectively – 'good

for ten years yet! I said only yesterday to Butrand – you know Butrand, he works on Le Blôt's Bon-Dieu place – "And that Madame Zidore: how is it with her, Butrand? I believe God has forgotten her here on earth." "It is n't that, your reverence," said Butrand, "but it's neither God nor the Devil that wants her!"'
And Père Antoine laughed with a jovial frankness that took all sting of ill-nature from his very pointed remarks.

Lalie did not reply when he spoke of her grandmother; she only pressed her lips firmly together, and picked nervously at the red bandana.

'I have come to ask, Monsieur Antoine,' she began, lower than she needed to speak – for Azenor had withdrawn at once to the far end of the porch – 'to ask if you will give me a little scrap of paper – a piece of writing for Monsieur Chartrand at the store over there. I want new shoes and stockings for Easter, and I have brought eggs to trade for them. He says he is willing, yes, if he was sure I would bring more every week till the shoes are paid for.'

With good-natured indifference, Père Antoine wrote the order that the girl desired. He was too familiar with distress to feel keenly for a girl who was able to buy Easter shoes and pay for them with eggs.

She went immediately away then, after shaking hands with the priest, and sending a quick glance of her pathetic eyes towards Azenor, who had turned when he heard her rise, and nodded when he caught the look. Through the vines he watched her cross the village street.

'How is it that you do not know Lalie, Azenor? You surely must have seen her pass your house often. It lies on her way to the Bon-Dieu.'

'No, I don't know her; I have never seen her,' the young man replied, as he seated himself – after the priest – and kept his eyes absently fixed on the store across the road, where he had seen her enter.

'She is the granddaughter of that Madame Izidore'—

'What! Ma'ame Zidore whom they drove off the island last winter?'

'Yes, yes. Well, you know, they say the old woman stole wood and things, – I don't know how true it is, – and destroyed people's property out of pure malice.'

'And she lives now on the Bon-Dieu?'

'Yes, on Le Blôt's place, in a perfect wreck of a cabin. You see, she gets it for nothing; not a negro on the place but has refused to live in it.'

'Surely, it can't be that old abandoned hovel near the swamp, that Michon occupied ages ago?'

'That is the one, the very one.'

'And the girl lives there with that old wretch?' the young man marvelled.

'Old wretch to be sure, Azenor. But what can you expect from a woman who never crosses the threshold of God's house – who even tried to hinder the child doing so as well? But I went to her. I said: "See here, Madame Zidore," – you know it's my way to handle such people without gloves, – "you may damn your soul if you choose," I told her, "that is a privilege which we all have; but none of us has a right to imperil the salvation of another. I want to see Lalie at mass hereafter on Sundays, or you will hear from me;" and I shook my stick under her nose. Since then the child has never missed a Sunday. But she is half starved, you can see that. You saw how shabby she is – how broken her shoes are? She is at Chartrand's now, trading for new ones with those eggs she brought, poor thing! There is no doubt of her being ill-treated. Butrand says he thinks Madame Zidore even beats the child. I don't know how true it is, for no power can make her utter a word against her grandmother.'

Azenor, whose face was a kind and sensitive one, had paled with distress as the priest spoke; and now at these final words he quivered as though he felt the sting of a cruel blow upon his own flesh.

But no more was said of Lalie, for Père Antoine drew the young man's attention to the carpenter-work which he wished to entrust to him. When they had talked the matter over in all its lengthy details, Azenor mounted his horse and rode away.

A moment's gallop carried him outside the village. Then came a half-mile strip along the river to cover. Then the lane to enter, in which stood his dwelling midway, upon a low, pleasant knoll.

As Azenor turned into the lane, he saw the figure of Lalie far ahead of him. Somehow he had expected to find her there, and he watched her again as he had done through Père Antoine's vines. When she passed his house, he wondered if she would turn to look at it. But she did not. How could she know it was his? Upon reaching it himself, he did not enter the yard, but stood there motionless, his eyes always fastened upon the girl's figure. He could not see, away off there, how coarse her garments were. She seemed, through the distance that divided them, as slim and delicate as a flower-stalk. He stayed till she reached the turn of the lane and disappeared into the woods.

Mass had not yet begun when Azenor tiptoed into church on Easter morning. He did not take his place with the congregation, but stood close to the holy-water font, and watched the people who entered.

Almost every girl who passed him wore a white mull, a dotted swiss, or a fresh-starched muslin at least. They were bright with ribbons that hung from their persons, and flowers that bedecked their hats. Some carried fans and cambric handkerchiefs. Most of them wore gloves, and were odorant of *poudre de riz* and nice toilet-waters; while all carried gay little baskets filled with Easter-eggs.

But there was one who came empty-handed, save for the worn prayer-book which she bore. It was Lalie, the veil upon her head, and wearing the blue print and cotton bodice which she had worn the day before.

He dipped his hand into the holy water when she came, and held it out to her, though he had not thought of doing this for the others. She touched his fingers with the tips of her own, making a slight inclination as she did so; and after a deep genuflection before the Blessed Sacrament, passed on to the side. He was not sure if she had known him. He knew she had not looked into his eyes, for he would have felt it.

He was angered against other young women who passed him, because of their flowers and ribbons, when she wore none. He himself did not care, but he feared she might, and watched her narrowly to see if she did.

But it was plain that Lalie did not care. Her face, as she seated herself, settled into the same restful lines it had worn yesterday, when she sat in Père Antoine's big chair. It seemed good to her to be there. Sometimes she looked up at the little coloured panes through which the Easter sun was streaming; then at the flaming candles, like stars; or at the embowered figures of Joseph and Mary, flanking the central tabernacle which shrouded the risen Christ. Yet she liked just as well to watch the young girls in their spring freshness, or to sensuously inhale the mingled odour of flowers and incense that filled the temple.

Lalie was among the last to quit the church. When she walked down the clean pathway that led from it to the road, she looked with pleased curiosity towards the groups of men and maidens who were gayly matching their Easter-eggs under the shade of the China-berry trees.

Azenor was among them, and when he saw her coming solitary down the path, he approached her and, with a smile, extended his hat, whose crown was quite lined with the pretty coloured eggs.

'You mus' of forgot to bring aiggs,' he said. 'Take some o' mine.'

'Non, merci,' she replied, flushing and drawing back.

But he urged them anew upon her. Much pleased, then, she bent her pretty head over the hat, and was evidently puzzled to make a selection among so many that were beautiful.

He picked out one for her, – a pink one, dotted with white clover-leaves.

'Yere,' he said, handing it to her, 'I think this is the pretties'; an' it look' strong too. I'm sho' it will break all of the res'.' And he playfully held out another, half-hidden in his fist, for her to try its strength upon. But she refused to. She would not risk the ruin of her pretty egg. Then she walked away, without once

Romantic Love

having noticed that the girls, whom Azenor had left, were looking curiously at her.

When he rejoined them, he was hardly prepared for their greeting; it startled him.

'How come you talk to that girl? She's real canaille, her,' was what one of them said to him.

'Who say' so? Who say she's canaille? If it's a man, I'll smash 'is head!' he exclaimed, livid. They all laughed merrily at this.

'An' if it's a lady, Azenor? W'at you goin' to do 'bout it?' asked another quizzingly.

'Tain' no lady. No lady would say that 'bout a po' girl, w'at she don't even know.'

He turned away, and emptying all his eggs into the hat of a little urchin who stood near, walked out of the churchyard. He did not stop to exchange another word with any one; neither with the men who stood all *endimanchés* before the stores, not the women who were mounting upon horses and into vehicles, or walking in groups to their homes.

He took a short cut across the cotton-field that extended back of the town, and walking rapidly, soon reached his home. It was a pleasant house of few rooms and many windows, with fresh air blowing through from every side; his workshop was beside it. A broad strip of greensward, studded here and there with trees, sloped down to the road.

Azenor entered the kitchen, where an amiable old black woman was chopping onion and sage at a table.

'Tranquiline,' he said abruptly, 'they's a young girl goin' to pass yere afta a w'ile. She's got a blue dress an' w'ite josie on, an' a veil on her head. W'en you see her, I want you to go to the road an' make her res' there on the bench, an' ask her if she don't want a cup o' coffee. I saw her go to communion, me; so she did n't eat any breakfas'. Eve'ybody else f'om out o' town, that went to communion, got invited somew'ere another. It's enough to make a person sick to see such meanness.'

'An' you want me ter go down to de gate, jis' so, an' ax 'er pineblank ef she wants some coffee?' asked the bewildered Tranquiline.

12

Love on the Bon-Dieu

'I don't care if you ask her poin' blank o' not; but you do like I say.' Tranquiline was leaning over the gate when Lalie came along.

'Howdy,' offered the woman.

'Howdy,' the girl returned.

'Did you see a yalla calf wid black spots a t'arin down de lane, missy?'

'Non; not yalla, an' not with black spot'. *Mais* I see one li'le w'ite calf tie by a rope, yonda 'roun' the ben'.

'Dat warn't hit. Dis heah one was yalla. I hope he done flung hisse'f down de bank an' broke his nake. Sarve 'im right! But whar you come f'om, chile? You look plum wo' out. Set down dah on dat bench, an' le' me fotch you a cup o' coffee.'

Azenor had already in his eagerness arranged a tray, upon which was a smoking cup of *café au lait*. He had buttered and jellied generous slices of bread, and was searching wildly for something when Tranquiline re-entered.

'W'at become o' that half of chicken-pie, Tranquiline, that was yere in the *garde manger* yesterday?'

'W'at chicken-pie? W'at *garde manger*?' blustered the woman.

'Like we got mo' 'en one *garde manger* in the house, Tranquiline!'

'You jis' like ole Ma'ame Azenor use' to be, you is! You 'spec' chicken-pie gwine las' etarnal? W'en some'pin done sp'ilt, I flings it 'way. Dat's me – dat's Tranquiline!'

So Azenor resigned himself, – what else could he do? – and sent the tray, incomplete, as he fancied it, out to Lalie.

He trembled as the thought of what he did; he, whose nerves were usually as steady as some piece of steel mechanism.

Would it anger her if she suspected? Would it please her if she knew? Would she say this or that to Tranquiline? And would Tranquiline tell him truly what she said – how she looked?

As it was Sunday, Azenor did not work that afternoon. Instead, he took a book out under the trees, as he often did, and sat reading it, from the first sound of the Vesper bell, that came faintly across the fields, till the Angelus. All that time! He turned many a page, yet in the end did not know what he had read. With

Romantic Love

his pencil he had traced 'Lalie' upon every margin, and was saying it softly to himself.

Another Sunday Azenor saw Lalie at mass – and again. Once he walked with her and showed her the short cut across the cotton field. She was very glad that day, and told him she was going to work – her grandmother said she might. She was going to hoe, up in the fields with Monsieur Le Blôt's hands. He entreated her not to; and when she asked his reason, he could not tell her, but turned and tore shyly and savagely at the elder-blossoms that grew along the fence.

Then they stopped where she was going to cross the fence from the field into the lane. He wanted to tell her that was his house which they could see not far away; but he did not dare to, since he had fed her there on the morning she was hungry.

'An' you say yo' gran'ma's goin' to let you work? She keeps you f'om workin', *donc?*' He wanted to question her about her grandmother, and could think of no other way to begin.

'Po' ole grand'mère!' she answered. 'I don' b'lieve she know mos' time w'at she's doin'. Sometime she say' I ain't no better an' one nigga, an' she fo'ce me to work. Then she say she know I'm goin' be one canaille like maman, an' she make me set down still, like she would want to kill me if I would move. Her, she on'y want' to be out in the wood', day an' night, day an' night. She ain' got her right head, po' grand'mère. I know she ain't.'

Lalie had spoken low and in jerks, as if every word gave her pain. Azenor could feel her distress as plainly as he saw it. He wanted to say something to her – to do something for her. But her mere presence paralyzed him into inactivity – except his pulses, that beat like hammers when he was with her. Such a poor, shabby little thing as she was, too!

'I'm goin' to wait yere nex' Sunday fo' you, Lalie,' he said, when the fence was between them. And he thought he had said something very daring.

But the next Sunday she did not come. She was neither at the appointed place of meeting in the lane, nor was she at mass. Her absence – so unexpected – affected Azenor like a calamity. Late in the afternoon, when he could stand the trouble and bewilderment of it no longer, he went and leaned over Père Antoine's fence. The priest was picking the slugs from his roses on the other side.

'That young girl from the Bon-Dieu,' said Azenor – 'she was not at mass today. I suppose her grandmother has forgotten your warning.'

'No,' answered the priest. 'The child is ill, I hear. Butrand tells me she has been ill for several days from overwork in the fields. I shall go out tomorrow to see about her. I would go today, if I could.'

'The child is ill,' was all Azenor heard or understood of Père Antoine's words. He turned and walked resolutely away, like one who determines suddenly upon action after meaningless hesitation.

He walked towards his home and past it, as if it were a spot that did not concern him. He went on down the lane and into the wood where he had seen Lalie disappear that day.

Here all was shadow, for the sun had dipped too low in the west to send a single ray through the dense foliage of the forest.

Now that he found himself on the way to Lalie's home, he strove to understand why he had not gone there before. He often visited other girls in the village and neighbourhood, – why not have gone to her, as well? The answer lay too deep in his heart for him to be more than half-conscious of it. Fear had kept him, – dread to see her desolate life face to face. He did not know how he could bear it.

But now he was going to her at last. She was ill. He would stand upon that dismantled porch that he could just remember. Doubtless Ma'ame Zidore would come out to know his will, and he would tell her that Père Antoine had sent to enquire how Mamzelle Lalie was. No! Why drag in Père Antoine? He would simply stand boldly and say, 'Ma'ame Zidore, I learn that Lalie is ill. I have come to know if it is true, and to see her, if I may.'

When Azenor reached the cabin where Lalie dwelt, all sign of day had vanished. Dusk had fallen swiftly after sunset. The moss that hung heavy from great live oak branches was making fantastic silhouettes against the eastern sky that the big, round moon was beginning to light. Off in the swamp beyond the bayou, hundreds of dismal voices were droning a lullaby. Upon the hovel itself, a stillness like death rested.

Oftener than once Azenor tapped upon the door, which was closed as well as it could be, without obtaining a reply. He finally approached one of the small unglazed windows, in which coarse mosquito-netting had been fastened, and looked into the room.

By the moonlight slanting in he could see Lalie stretched upon a bed; but of Ma'ame Zidore there was no sign. 'Lalie!' he called softly. 'Lalie!'

The girl sightly moved her head upon the pillow. Then he boldly opened the door and entered.

Upon a wretched bed, over which was spread a cover of patched calico, Lalie lay, her frail body only half concealed by the single garment that was upon it. One hand was plunged beneath her pillow; the other, which was free, he touched. It was as hot as flame; so was her head. He knelt sobbing upon the floor beside her, and called her his love and his soul. He begged her to speak a word to him, – to look at him. But she only muttered disjointedly that the cotton was all turning to ashes in the fields, and the blades of the corn were in flames.

If he was choked with love and grief to see her so, he was moved by anger as well; rage against himself, against Père Antoine, against the people upon the plantation and in the village, who had so abandoned a helpless creature to misery and maybe death. Because she had been silent – had not lifted her voice in complaint – they believed she suffered no more than she could bear.

But surely the people could not be utterly without heart. There must be one somewhere with the spirit of Christ. Père Antoine would tell him of such a one, and he would carry Lalie to her, – out of this atmosphere of death. He was in haste to be gone with her. He fancied every moment of delay was a fresh danger threatening her life.

He folded the rude bed-cover over Lalie's naked limbs, and lifted her in his arms. She made no resistance. She seemed only loath to withdraw her hand from beneath the pillow. When she did, he saw that she held lightly but firmly clasped in her encircling fingers the pretty Easter-egg he had given her! He uttered a low cry of exultation as the full significance of this came over him. If she had hung for hours upon his neck telling him that she loved him, he could not have known it more surely than by this sign. Azenor felt as if some mysterious bond had all at once drawn them heart to heart and made them one.

No need now to go from door to door begging admittance for her. She was his. She belonged to him. He knew now where her place was, whose roof must shelter her, and whose arms protect her.

So Azenor, with his loved one in his arms, walked through the forest, surefooted as a panther. Once, as he walked, he could hear in the distance the weird chant which Ma'ame Zidore was crooning – to the moon, maybe – as she gathered her wood.

Once, where the water was trickling cool through the rocks, he stopped to lave Lalie's hot cheeks and hands and forehead. He had not once touched his lips to her. But now, when a sudden great fear came upon him because she did not know him, instinctively he pressed his lips upon hers that were parched and burning. He held them there till hers were soft and pliant from the healthy moisture of his own.

Then she knew him. She did not tell him so, but her stiffened fingers relaxed their tense hold upon the Easter bauble. It fell to the ground as she twined her arm around his neck; and he understood.

'Stay close by her, Tranquiline,' said Azenor, when he had laid Lalie upon his own couch at home. 'I'm goin' for the doctor en' for Père Antoine. Not because she is goin' to die,' he added hastily, seeing the awe that crept into the woman's face at the mention of the priest. 'She is goin' to live! Do you think I would let my wife die, Tranquiline?'

By Grand Central Station I Sat Down and Wept

Elizabeth Smart

O the water of love that floods everything over, so that there is nothing the eye sees that is not covered in. There is no angle the world can assume which the love in my eye cannot make into a symbol of love. Even the precise geometry of his hand, when I gaze at it, dissolves me into water and I flow away in a flood of love.

Everything flows like the Mississippi over a devastated earth, which drinks unsurfeited, and augments the liquid with waterfalls of gratitude; which raises a sound of praise to deafen all doubters forever; to burst their shamed eardrums with the roar of proof, louder than bombs or screams or the inside ticking of remorse. Not all the poisonous tides of the blood I have spilt can influence these tidals of love.

But how can I go through the necessary daily motions, when such an intense fusion turns the world to water?

The overflow drenches all my implements of trivial intercourse. I stare incomprehension at the simplest question from a stranger, standing as if bewitched, half-smiling, like an idiot, feeling this fiery fluid spill out of my eyes.

I am possessed by love and have no options.

When the Ford rattles up to the door, five minutes (five years) late, and he walks across the lawn under the pepper-trees, I stand behind the gauze curtains, unable to move to meet him, or to speak, as I turn to liquid to invade his every orifice when he opens the door. More single-purposed than the new bird, all mouth with his one want, I close my eyes and tremble, anticipating the heaven of actual touch.

When we lie near the swimming pool in the sun, he comes through the bamboo bushes like land emerging from chaos. But

I am the land, and he is the face upon the waters. He is the moon upon the tides, the dew, the rain, all seeds and all the honey of love. My bones are crushed like the bamboo-trees. I am the earth the plants grow through. But when they sprout I also will be a god.

And there is so much for me, I am suddenly so rich, and I have done nothing to deserve it, to be so overloaded. All after such a desert. All after I had learnt to say, I am nothing, and I deserve nothing.

The thick pines drop globular cones; the dishevelled palms, with their pantaloons falling down their trunks say,

It has happened, the miracle has arrived, everything begins today, everything you touch is born; the new moon attended by two enormous stars; the sunny day fading with a glow to exhilaration; all the paraphernalia of existence, all my sad companions of these last twenty years, the pots and pans in Mrs Wurtle's kitchen, ribbons of streets, wilted geraniums, thin children's legs, all the world solicits me with joy, leaps at me electrically, claiming its birth at last.

When we tear ourselves out of the night and come into the kitchen, Mrs Wurtle says, 'Romance, eh?', but she smiles, she turns away her head, and when we kiss behind her back as we help her dry the dishes, she says, 'Oh, you two love-birds, go on out again!'

What is going to happen? Nothing. For everything has happened. All time is now, and time can do no better. Nothing can ever be more than now, and before this nothing was. There are no minor facts in life, there is only the one tremendous one.

We can include the world in our love, and no irritations can disrupt it, not even envy.

Mr Wurtle, sitting on the sofa late at night, says, with a legal air, 'Then I have it from you there is such a thing as Love?' I lean upon the cushion, faint from this few hours' separation, but I sigh, 'Yes, oh, yes,' and then, as if he were describing other worlds, diminutive, so petty I smother them in pity, he describes his intrigues, he bandies the Word that Was in the Beginning.

Romantic Love

But the noise of my inside seas, the dazzle of this cataclysmic birth of love in me, cannot hear clearly what he says. To make a response is like rousing a heavy sleeper who longs to remain asleep. I smile, but I am in a trance, there is no reality but love.

I cannot hear beneath his subtle words the beginning of the world's antagonism: the hatred of the mediocre for all miracles. All I want is for everyone to go away and leave me a thousand lives in which to muse, only to muse, on this state of completion.

I was taunted so long. The meaning fluttered above my head, always out of reach. Now it has come to rest in me. It has pierced the very centre of the circle. I love, love, love –, but he is also all things: the night, the resilient mornings, the tall poinsettias and hydrangeas, the lemon trees, the residential palms, the fruit and vegetables in gorgeous rows, the birds in the pepper-tree, the sun on the swimming pool.

There is no room for pity, of anything. In a bleeding heart I should find only exhilaration in the richness of the red.

Once I skulked wistfully through dim streets, aching after this unknown, hoping to pass by unnoticed in my drab dress and lopsided shoes with high heels, hoping, thus surreptitiously, to come upon it. But I was afraid, I was timid, and I did not believe, I hoped. I thought it would be like a bird in the hand, not a wild sea that treated me like flotsam.

But I have become a part of the earth: I am one of its waves flooding and leaping. I am the same tune now as the trees, hummingbirds, sky, fruits, vegetables in rows. I am all or any of these. I can metamorphose at will.

Do you need some joy or love? Are you sodden leaves in some forsaken yard? Are you deserted or cold or starved or paralyzed or blind? Handfuls and handfuls for you, and to spare!

Make them up into bedsocks, teacosies, cushions against the cold, for their electricity is perpetual warmth, and can contaminate everything, and build at one touch a new and adorable world.

This is Today. This is where all roads strove to lead, all feet to attain. What are the world's problems and sorrows and errors? I am as at sea, and as ignorant and mystified, as the first day I ever saw algebra.

There are no problems, no sorrows or errors: they join in the urging song that everything sings. This is the state of the angels, that spend their hours only singing the praises of the Lord. Just to lie savouring is enough life. Is enough.

Even in transient coffee-shops and hotels, or the gloom of taverns, the crooning of Bing Crosby out of a jukebox, and the bar-tender clanking glasses, achieve a perfect identity, a high round note of their own flavour, that makes me tearful with the gratitude of reception.

And merely his hand under those shabby tables, or guiding me across the stubble of the fields, makes my happiness as inexhaustible as the ocean, and as warm and comfortable as the womb.

When I saw a horde of cats gathering at a railway terminus to feed on a fish-head thrown near the tracks, I felt, It is the lavishness of my feelings that feeds even the waifs and strays. There are not too many bereaved or wounded but I can comfort them, and those 5,000,000 who never stop dragging their feet and bundles and babies with bloated bellies across Europe, are not too many or too benighted for me to say, Here's a world of hope, I can spare a whole world for each and every one, like a rich lady dispensing bags of candy at a poor children's Christmas feast.

I can compress the whole Mojave Desert into one word of inspiration, or call all America to obey my whim, like the waiter standing to take my order. I am delirious with power and invulnerability.

Take away what is supposed to be enviable: the silver brushes with my name, the long gown, the car, the hundred suitors, poise in a restaurant – I am still richer than the greediest heart could conceive, able to pour my overflowing benevolence over even the tight-mouthed look. Take everything I have, or could have, or anything the world could offer, I am still empress of a new-found land, that neither Columbus nor Cortez could have equalled, even in their instigating dream.

Set me as a seal upon thine heart, as a seal upon thine arm, for love is strong as death.

The Song of Solomon

The Bible

The *Song of Solomon* **Chapter 5, v. 8–16 and Chapter 6, v. 1–13.**

CHAPTER 5

8 I charge you, O daughters of Jerusalem, if ye find my beloved, that ye tell him, that I *am* sick of love.

9 What *is* thy beloved more than *another* beloved, O thou fairest among women? What *is* thy beloved more than *another* beloved, that thou dost so charge us?

10 My beloved *is* white and ruddy, the chiefest among ten thousand.

11 His head *is as* the most fine gold, his locks *are* bushy, *and* black as a raven.

12 His eyes *are* as *the eyes* of doves by the rivers of waters, washed with milk, *and* fitly set.

13 His cheeks *are* as a bed of spices, *as* sweet flowers: his lips *like* lilies, dropping sweet smelling myrrh.

14 His hands *are as* gold rings set with the beryl: his belly *is as* bright ivory overlaid *with* sapphires.

15 His legs *are as* pillars of marble, set upon sockets of fine gold: his countenance *is* as Lĕb'-ă-non, excellent as the cedars.

16 His mouth *is* most sweet: yea, he *is* altogether lovely. This *is* my beloved, and this *is* my friend, O daughters of Jerusalem.

CHAPTER 6

Whither is thy beloved gone, O thou fairest among women? whither is thy beloved turned aside? that we may seek him with thee.

2 My beloved is gone down into his garden, to the beds of spices, to feed in the gardens, and to gather lilies.

3 I *am* my beloved's, and my beloved *is* mine: he feedeth among the lilies.

4 Thou *art* beautiful, O my love, as Tĭr'-zăh, comely as Jerusalem, terrible as *an army* with banners.

5 Turn away thine eyes from me, for they have overcome me: thy hair *is* as a flock of goats that appear from Gilead.

6 Thy teeth *are* as a flock of sheep which go up from the washing, where-of every one beareth twins, and *there is* not one barren among them.

7 As a piece of a pomegranate *are* thy temples within thy locks.

8 There are threescore queens, and fourscore concubines, and virgins without number.

9 My dove, my undefiled is *but* one; she *is* the *only* one of her mother, she *is* the choice *one* of her that bare her. The daughters saw her, and blessed her; *yea*, the queens and the concubines, and they praised her.

10 Who *is* she *that* looketh forth as the morning, fair as the moon, clear as the sun, *and* terrible as *an army* with banners?

11 I went down into the garden of nuts to see the fruits of the valley *and* to see whether the vine flourished, *and* the pomegranates budded.

12 Or ever I was aware, my soul made me *like* the chariots of Ăm-mĭn'-ă-dĭb.

13 Return, return, O Shû'-lă-mite; return, return, that we may look upon thee. What will ye see in the Shû'-lă-mite? As it were the company of two armies.

Right from the Heart

Stephen Burgen

The language of love is gushing forth as St Valentine's Day nears. Declarations decorating cards and classified ads are as likely to spout from John Donne as the Andrews Sisters. It suggests that no other language is quite as exhaustive, if not exhausted. In the words of Elizabeth Barrett Browning: How do I love thee? Let me count the ways.

Come live with me and be my main squeeze. My precious, my treasure, be my Valentine. My cherie amour, my darling, my dearest; my old flame has gone out now I'm carrying a torch for you. Don't change your hair for me, not if you care for me, I love you just the way you are. Say you'll be mine, sweet chuck, for ever and ever. If loving you is wrong, I don't want to be right.

Where the bee sups, there sup I, my honey, at your sweet lips. Oh sugar pie honeybunch, you know that I love you. It's you, babycakes, that I adore and cherish, my sugar dumpling, my honey-dripper, my honeysuckle rose. I could drink a case of you and still be on my feet. Oh baby, baby, oh baby, I'm crazy about you. Since the first time ever I saw your face I've had a crush on you; you swept me off my feet and I knew you were the one I'd been dreaming of and now I'm hopelessly devoted to you.

Being your slave, what should I do but be your toy, your puppet on a string. I've got you under my skin, come rain or come shine, and have got to get you into my life. For you I'd get the top brick from a chimney and bring you the moon and the stars because you're more than a number in my little red book. You make my motor run and my thermometer rise; when we kiss, oooh, you give me fever so let's do it. I'm a fool for love, so why not take all of me. I'll be your plaything if you'd just say I'm yours and yours alone, your one and only, your number one, because I don't want to be your sidetrack till your mainline comes along.

I bless the day I found you, earth angel, now I believe in miracles and the moment I wake up I say a little prayer for you. You are my sunshine and heaven must have sent you into my arms

Romantic Love

because when ever you're near I hear a symphony. My heart went boom when you crossed that room, zing went the strings of my heart and then I got it bad and that ain't good. When we're together, oh dreamboat, I'm in paradise, I'm bewitched, bothered and bewildered, so do do that voodoo that you do so well. I'm so smitten, so mad about you, liebchen, all I think about is you because I'm stuck like glue, stuck on you so be the one, be my teddy bear.

Speak low, if you speak, of love, but you can ring my bell whenever you want to because my lovelight is always burning and my heart is on fire; like a summer with a thousand Julys you intoxicate my soul with your eyes, just please don't sit under the apple tree with anyone else but me. I only have eyes for you so let's go steady, please wear my ring. I'll be your Dixie chicken if you'll be my Tennessee lamb. Be my partner, my inamorata, my special friend, my paramour, my better half, my light luggage of essentials. Be my significant other.

The End of Something

Ernest Hemingway

In the old days Hortons Bay was a lumbering town. No one who lived in it was out of sound of the big saws in the mill by the lake. Then one year there were no more logs to make lumber. The lumber schooners came into the bay and were loaded with the cut of the mill that stood stacked in the yard. All the piles of lumber were carried away. The big mill building had all its machinery that was removable taken out and hoisted on board one of the schooners by the men who had worked in the mill. The schooner moved out of the bay toward the open lake carrying the two great saws, the travelling carriage that hurled the logs against the revolving, circular saws, and all the rollers, wheels, belts, and iron piled on a hull-deep load of lumber. Its open hold covered with canvas and lashed tight, the sails of the schooner filled and it moved out into the open lake, carrying with it everything that had made the mill a mill and Hortons Bay a town.

The one-storey bunk houses, the eating-house, the company store, the mill offices, and the big mill itself stood deserted in the acres of sawdust that covered the swampy meadow by the shore of the bay.

Ten years later there was nothing of the mill left except the broken white limestone of its foundations showing through the swampy second growth as Nick and Marjorie rowed along the shore. They were trolling along the edge of the channel bank where the bottom dropped off suddenly from sandy shallows to twelve feet of dark water. They were trolling on their way to the point to set night-lines for rainbow trout.

'There's our old ruin, Nick,' Marjorie said.

Nick, rowing, looked at the white stone in the green trees.

'There it is,' he said.

'Can you remember when it was a mill?' Marjorie asked.

'I can just remember,' Nick said.

'It seems more like a castle,' Marjorie said.

Nick said nothing. They rowed on out of sight of the mill, following the shore line. Then Nick cut across the bay.

'They aren't striking,' he said.

'No,' Marjorie said. She was intent on the rod all the time they trolled, even when she talked. She loved to fish. She loved to fish with Nick.

Close beside the boat a big trout broke the surface of the water. Nick pulled hard on one oar so the boat would turn and the bait spinning far behind would pass where the trout was feeding. As the trout's back came up out of the water the minnows jumped wildly. They sprinkled the surface like a handful of shot thrown into the water. Another trout broke water, feeding on the other side of the boat.

'They're feeding,' Marjorie said.

'But they won't strike,' Nick said.

He rowed the boat around to troll past both the feeding fish, then headed it for the point. Marjorie did not reel in until the boat touched the shore.

They pulled the boat up the beach and Nick lifted out a pail of live perch. The perch swam in the water in the pail. Nick caught three of them with his hands and cut their heads off and skinned them while Marjorie chased with her hands in the bucket, finally caught a perch, cut its head off, and skinned it. Nick looked at her fish.

'You don't want to take the ventral fin out,' he said. 'It'll be all right for bait but it's better with the ventral fin in.'

He hooked each of the skinned perch through the tail. There were two hooks attached to a leader on each rod. Then Marjorie rowed the boat out over the channel-bank, holding the line in her teeth, and looking toward Nick, who stood on the shore holding the rod and letting the line run out from the reel.

'That's about right,' he called.

'Should I let it drop?' Marjorie called back, holding the line in her hand.

The End of Something

'Sure. Let it go.' Marjorie dropped the line overboard and watched the baits go down through the water.

She came in with the boat and ran the second line out the same way. Each time Nick set a heavy slab of driftwood across the butt of the rod to hold it solid and propped it up at an angle with a small slab. He reeled in the slack so the line ran taut out to where the bait rested on the sandy floor of the channel and set the click on the reel. When a trout, feeding on the bottom, took the bait it would run with it, taking line out of the reel in a rush and making the reel sing with the click on.

Marjorie rowed up the point a little way so she would not disturb the line. She pulled hard on the oars and the boat went way up the beach. Little waves came in with it. Marjorie stepped out of the boat and Nick pulled the boat high up the beach.

'What's the matter, Nick?' Marjorie asked.

'I don't know,' Nick said, getting wood for a fire.

They made a fire with driftwood. Marjorie went to the boat and brought a blanket. The evening breeze blew the smoke toward the point, so Marjorie spread the blanket out between the fire and the lake.

Marjorie sat on the blanket with her back to the fire and waited for Nick. He came over and sat down beside her on the blanket. In back of them was the close second-growth timber of the point and in front was the bay with the mouth of Hortons Creek. It was not quite dark. The firelight went as far as the water. They could both see the two steel rods at an angle over the dark water. The fire glinted on the reels.

Marjorie unpacked the basket of supper.

'I don't feel like eating,' said Nick.

'Come on and eat, Nick.'

'All right.'

They ate without talking, and watched the two rods and the firelight in the water.

'There's going to be a moon tonight,' said Nick. He looked across the bay to the hills that were beginning to sharpen against the sky. Beyond the hills he knew the moon was coming up.

Romantic Love

'I know it,' Marjorie said happily.

'You know everything,' Nick said.

'Oh, Nick, please cut it out! Please, please don't be that way!'

'I can't help it,' Nick said. 'You do. You know everything. That's the trouble. You know you do.'

Marjorie did not say anything.

'I've taught you everything. You know you do. What don't you know, anyway?'

'Oh, shut up.' Marjorie said. 'There comes the moon.'

They sat on the blanket without touching each other and watched the moon rise.

'You don't have to talk silly,' Marjorie said. 'What's really the matter?'

'I don't know.'

'Of course you know.'

'No, I don't.'

'Go on and say it.'

Nick looked on at the moon, coming up over the hills.

'It isn't fun any more.'

He was afraid to look at Marjorie. Then he looked at her. She sat there with her back toward him. He looked at her back. 'It isn't fun any more. Not any of it.'

She didn't say anything. He went on. 'I feel as though everything was gone to hell inside of me. I don't know, Marge. I don't know what to say.'

He looked on at her back.

'Isn't love any fun?' Marjorie said.

'No,' Nick said. Marjorie stood up. Nick sat there, his head in his hands.

'I'm going to take the boat,' Marjorie called to him. 'You can walk back around the point.'

'All right,' Nick said. 'I'll push the boat off for you.'

'You don't need to,' she said. She was afloat in the boat on the water with the moonlight on it. Nick went back and lay down with his face in the blanket by the fire. He could hear Marjorie rowing on the water.

The End of Something

He lay there for a long time. He lay there while he heard Bill come into the clearing walking around through the woods. He felt Bill coming up to the fire. Bill didn't touch him, either.

'Did she go all right?' Bill said.

'Yes,' Nick said, lying, his face on the blanket.

'Have a scene?'

'No, there wasn't any scene.'

'How do you feel?'

'Oh, go away, Bill! Go away for a while.'

Bill selected a sandwich from the lunch basket and walked over to have a look at the rods.

Jealous Love
Roman Fever

Edith Wharton
(adapted for radio by Janet Goodwyn)

Characters

Mrs Alida Slade — *Wealthy widow of an American international lawyer, on holiday in Rome*
Mrs Grace Ansley — *Widow from New York also on holiday in Rome*
Jenny Slade — *Quiet and considerate daughter of Mrs Slade, aged 25*
Barbara Ansley — *Lively and dynamic daughter of Grace Ansley, also 25*
Lydia/English Lady — *Guest at party/customer in cafe*
Waiter/American Man — *At cafe/guest at party*
Female 1 }
Female 2 } *Guests at party*

(Bring up music. Hold then fade down and mix with exterior: terrace restaurant in Rome, Spring 1925)

1. **Mrs Ansley:** I'm so glad we all met up in this way... it's such a treat for Barbara to have someone of her own age to go about with... isn't that right, my dear?
2. **Barbara:** *(Teasingly)* What you really mean, darling, is that you're indescribably relieved that you don't have to make even so much as a pretence of chaperoning me around Rome now that Jenny is here. You can sit on your terrace, with your eternal knitting, from dawn till dusk.

1. **Mrs Slade:** Your mother and I would be glad to accompany you, Barbara, I'm sure. Do you have any plans for this afternoon, Jenny?
2. **Jenny:** Yes, I think so, but it's a little soon after lunch for you to be rushing about, mother. Why don't you take the afternoon to relax; enjoy the view... it is your favourite. Come on, let's go, Babs.

(Exclamations of goodbye, kisses, chairs moving, etc.)

3. **Mrs Ansley:** You will take care, my dears. Oh... I know you don't take any notice of me, Barbara, but I'm sure Jenny knows what I mean... I think those young Italian aviators we met at the Embassy invited them to fly to Tarquinia for tea. I suppose they'll want to wait and fly back by moonlight.
4. **Mrs Slade:** Moonlight... moonlight – I'm surprised it still plays such a part in their plans. Do you suppose that they're as sentimental as we were? Oh... there they go... beneath the terrace, look...
5. **Barbara:** *(Distant but clearly audible)* Do come on, Jenny... The young things are quite happy to be left to their knitting...
6. **Jenny:** Oh, Babs... really...
7. **Barbara:** Our poor mothers haven't much else to do, after all.

(All noise of lively conversation and laughter fades into the distance)

8. **Mrs Ansley:** I am sorry, Alida, I'm sure Barbara didn't mean to be rude – you see I do have my knitting... *(Apologetic laugh)*... it's my poor attempt to fill some of the time this new system of parenting has given us for our own. Barbara seems rather to subscribe to the collective modern idea of mothers and I suppose I've never done anything to disprove it. Here we are looking at the most exquisite view Rome has to offer and I don't feel stimulated beyond my daughter's view of me.
9. **Mrs Slade:** *(With a laugh that is a little aggrieved)* Ah, Rome is such a wonderful sight in Spring but I suppose we will have to get used to it representing our past as well as it's own...

Jealous Love

1. **Mrs Slade (contd):** ...why does one still expect the sap to rise I wonder? Perhaps I'm not ready to be written off yet...
2. **Mrs Ansley:** I'm sure Barbara didn't mean...
3. **Mrs Slade:** No matter, no matter... since Delphin's death I have rather taken a back seat, as the younger generation might say... there was always so much excitement, so much activity in the social sense whenever Delphin and I went abroad. It's rather odd to have time for contemplation now... after all it is the most beautiful view in the world.
4. **Mrs Ansley:** It always will be to me.

(FX nearby – a waiter clattering crocks and cups, scraping tables and chairs and generally making ostentatious clearing up sounds)

Oh, do you think that waiter wants us to leave? He seems to be wondering...

5. **Mrs Slade:** I'll cure him of wondering... where did I put my bag? (*Calls*) Waiter!
6. **Waiter:** (*Approaches*) Madame wishes something?
7. **Mrs Slade:** Yes – my friend and I are old lovers of Rome and would like to pass the rest of the afternoon with the view... if it won't disturb your service, of course.
8. **Waiter:** You are most welcome (*FX coins*) ah, thank you Madame... most welcome... if Madame would care to remain for dinner... full moon tonight – a beautiful sight over the city (*Moves off*) you will enjoy.
9. **Mrs Ansley:** That moon again...
10. **Mrs Slade:** (*Snappishly*) Yes... I don't know why he thinks I should be interested unless he expects the girls to come back with those young men... the one who is the pilot... he's a Marchese I understand, one of the Campolieri family?...
11. **Mrs Ansley:** (*Vaguely*) I believe so... yes... They're very young – the girls – despite what they say and do... just as we were when we first came to Rome.
12. **Mrs Slade:** Do you suppose they know as little as we did? – of themselves or each other? When we first met here we

Roman Fever

1. **Mrs Slade (contd):** were younger than our girls are now. How close the concerns of that time still are... the preoccupations of youth never die... despite the years that separate us from the girls and from our young selves... The years of marriage, twenty five years of my life with Delphin seem to have less reality than my girlhood, our girlhood, the time we spent in Rome. It's an effort to recall the married years even though they were such wonderful years; being a wife was so fulfilling... (*Fades*)... (*Thinking aloud*) Life with Delphin was so truly satisfactory, our marriage was such a success as a partnership. Together we were outstanding in New York society; I made myself socially effective whilst Delphin made his reputation in business... (*Fades out*)

(*Fade up background noise of a cocktail party. Voices are heard above the general clamour*)

2. **American Man:** (*Approaches*) Alida, darling! How wonderfully well you look!
3. **Mrs Slade:** Thank you... really, I enjoy these little soirées so much I'm sure they keep me happy... and that's the secret of well-being, after all. So many people seem to make themselves needlessly unhappy... don't you think so?
4. **American Man:** Yes,... of course... where did we last meet?... London wasn't it? I don't know how you keep it up – gadding about all over the world... Delphin has been working in Paris lately, hasn't he?
5. **Mrs Slade:** Yes, yes... we're just back from France... I'm merely a part of his procession, you know... I'm expected to organize impromptu little entertainments like this at a moment's notice since his business became international. I never thought, when I married a lawyer, that he would have the world as his practice.
6. **American Man:** Nonsense, my dear. With you to support him no wonder he's so successful. We all know that it's you who has made him what he is today. You put up such a good show together socially, and that's what people like to see...

1. **American Man (contd):** ...and even more important, that's what the business community likes to see. They want to feel that they've got a good, solid family man to look after their public reputation for them... and you two certainly present a united front to the world...

    (*Fade down party background under*)

2. **Mrs Slade:** (*Revery continued*) Yes... we were really both professional people... Delphin and I... marriage was my profession and I made Delphin proud of me in all sorts of ways...

    (*Bring up background of party*)

3. **English voice:** You mean that handsome woman... the one with the good clothes and eyes is Mrs Slade?... the Slade's wife? Really? The wives of celebrities are usually such frumps...

    (*Bring up background, then lower under*)

4. **Lydia:** (*Off*) Alida... Oh Alida... over here...
5. **Mrs Slade:** Lydia... how are you? (*Emphatic*) How many years is it?... My goodness...
6. **Lydia:** Far too many to count, my dear; let's just see. We were in Rome for ten years at the Consulate, and then in Cairo for six – all but three months – and Peter has been Ambassador now for just as many again. I told you there were too many to count. How are all the old crowd?... You know from our Roman winter together... I can see by looking at you how well you are... and Delphin the same... Ah... I'm sure he was here just now... never mind... as I was saying... We hear about you all the time from our visitors from home, you know... Oh, yes, we have a constant stream of Americans through the Embassy... what a wonderful life you lead, you two. Your receptions are very famous... yes, yes, they are... famous the world over. How is dear Grace? I remember what a lovely girl she was... is she still as charming or has marriage changed all that?... I don't see her here.

(*Lower background under*)

1. **Mrs Slade:** (*Revery continued*) How strange to remember Grace just then. She did seem to intrude upon one's memories rather more than she seemed to deserve. Look at her... knitting... Sitting on a terrace, even a Roman terrace, with Grace Ansley is certainly a come-down from the sort of life I led with Delphin. Being the Slade's wife was no preparation for being Slade's widow. (*Slight pause*) Didn't people realize?... didn't they understand?... I'm not finished yet... Oh, yes... I heard young Barbara Ansley talking about me earlier...

(*Edge out*)

(*Fade up*)

2. **Barbara:** Oh, Jenny... You know we don't want the mothers trailing around with us. They'd be sure to reminisce about (*Mocking voice*) 'the old days'... 'when we were girls in Rome'... and tell us again how lucky we are to be so free and so on and so on. I'd rather we were free of them entirely... I know I couldn't keep a straight face if we had another lecture in the Colosseum on Roman Fever and its role in American History... (*Fades*)

3. **Mrs Slade:** (*Revery continued*) How Grace and that nullity Horace Ansley ever produced that whirlwind Barbara was a complete mystery. They were always so respectable... especially when respectability was out of fashion... For years Delphin and I lived on the opposite side of the same street from Horace and Grace... but it grew so tedious, the chronicles of travel, of anniversaries, of curtain renewals... I watched it all with a growing sense of boredom. The safe, irreproachable Ansleys were so predictable that by the time Delphin made his big coup on Wall Street we were ready for a change of scene. When we bought our place in Upper Park Avenue I was certainly glad to leave the Ansleys behind... they made me feel so... well... so watched... I even made

Jealous Love

1. **Mrs Slade (contd):** a social hit with a joke about poor Grace... at a women's luncheon. (*Edge out*)

   (*Fade up luncheon background – female voices, glasses and cutlery*)

2. **Female One:** But won't you be sorry to leave the house, Alida? You've lived there all your married life, haven't you? Don't you have friends... old friends, in the neighbourhood? Grace Ansley lives right across from you, doesn't she?

   (*Background chat lessens a little as the whole party listens to the exchange*)

3. **Mrs Slade:** Oh really, my dear, that's a good reason for moving. I'd rather live opposite a speakeasy for a change...at least one might see it raided.

   (*Much hilarity and 'Oh Alidas' from miscellaneous voices*)

4. **Female Two:** Ooh – can you just imagine Horace and Grace being raided?...drinking tea with the raiding party emptying the teapot to try and find the gin!

   (*Laughter again and fade lunch background*)

5. **Mrs Slade:** (*Revery continued*) Had Grace ever heard the joke repeated? Well, if she had she'd never shown any sign of it. Grace had so little spirit, so little imagination... but she always seemed to have been there. To be a presence in my life despite the fact that after the move we never saw each other... except when the boy died, of course... Grace came then... (*Clean out*)

   (*Fade up large silent salon*)

6. **Mrs Ansley:** I'm so sorry Alida, so terribly sorry... so young... such a loss...
7. **Mrs Slade:** (*Stiffly*) That's alright Grace. Thank you for coming. Very kind of you. I'm afraid Delphin can see no-one. I'm sure you understand.

(Edge out)

1. **Mrs Slade:** *(Revery continued)* Yes, Grace had come then... It was too painful to recall, especially now that Delphin was gone as well as the son who had seemed to inherit all his gifts... There is really nothing left for me to do except to mother Jenny and Jenny doesn't give me much opportunity to do even that... not like Babs Ansley... Oh Barbara doesn't have the same kind of tranquil beauty that Grace had when she was young... but Barbara is more effective... has got more edge, as they say. How Grace can sit there with that girl to worry over... even though she's out with Jenny... my dear, safe Jenny... a rare creature indeed... an extremely pretty girl who somehow manages to make youth and prettiness as safe as their absence. Perhaps my own youth might have lasted a little bit longer if only Jenny truly needed me, if she involved me in a young life... If Jenny fell in love with the wrong man...and had to be watched, schemed over, outmanœuvred, rescued. But no...as luck would have it... Jenny does the watching, keeps me out of draughts, remembers to give me my tonic... there can be no doubt about it, Jenny makes me feel old. I don't want to be made so comfortable... Jenny would be better advised to look out for herself a bit more... Babs Ansley only wants my girl for a foil... she will come back engaged to that Campolieri boy and my Jenny will be left out... Babs will have it all... and still Grace can knit... even in the face of this view – The Palace of the Caesars – there's nothing in her face... nothing...

(Bring up terrace background exterior)

(Ringing of church bells for five o'clock as the noise of the restaurant and the city gradually re-establishes itself)

2. **Mrs Ansley:** I'm afraid that's five o'clock already my dear... I felt so comfortable just sitting here quietly with you I scarcely realized... it's so lovely... so full of old memories... not that I mean to revive painful feelings for you, you must feel a great many sadnesses as you look back.

1. **Mrs Slade:** (*Abruptly*) I don't know what you mean I'm sure.
2. **Mrs Ansley:** (*After a moment's hesitation*) Ah... no... there's Bridge at the Embassy at five.
3. **Mrs Slade:** (*Distractedly*) Bridge did you say? No... no... not unless you want to... I don't think I will you know. (*Pause before Mrs Slade begins to speak again*) (*Slowly*) I was just thinking about the different things Rome means to each generation of travellers. To our grandmothers it meant Roman Fever... to our mothers only sentimental dangers – how we were guarded at every turn! What can it mean to our daughters? No more danger than in the middle of Main Street... How much they're missing with their wonderful new freedom they have no idea!
4. **Mrs Ansley:** Yes, how we were guarded.
5. **Mrs Slade:** Well, I'm sure we all had our own ways of escape. I always used to think that our mothers had a much more difficult task than our grandmothers. When Roman Fever stalked the streets it must have been easy – comparatively, of course – for them to gather the girls in as the dangerous hour of darkness drew near; but when you and I were young, with the beauty of Rome, yes the beauty of Rome under the moonlight calling to us and the excitement of disobedience thrown in... well, there was no worst risk than catching cold during the cool hour of sunset for them to threaten us with. (*deliberate pause*) I suppose your illness might have borne their worst fears out, though... Your illness did start with a chill, didn't it?
6. **Mrs Ansley:** Yes. So the doctors said. (*Mutters*) One, two, three – slip two; yes, there's certainly nothing I can find to say to Barbara to keep her in; nor, I suppose, do I want to, really.
7. **Mrs Slade:** (*With a sardonic laugh*) Yes, your Babs certainly carries everything before her. That Campolieri boy is one of the best matches in Rome. Don't look so innocent my dear, you know he is. I've been wondering, ever so

1. **Mrs Slade (contd):** respectfully you understand, how two such exemplary characters as you and Horace ever managed to produce anything quite so dynamic. (*She laughs again*)
2. **Mrs Ansley:** (*Mutters*) Eighty-one, eighty-two – the end of a row... I'm sure you over-rate Barbara, my dear.
3. **Mrs Slade:** No, I don't. I appreciate her and perhaps I even envy you. Oh, my Jenny is perfect; if I were an invalid – well I think I'd rather be in Jenny's hands than anyone else's. But there are times... but there! I always wanted a brilliant daughter... I've never quite understood why I got an angel instead.
4. **Mrs Ansley:** Babs is an angel too.
5. **Mrs Slade:** Of course... but with rainbow wings. (*Pause*) Well, they're flying away with their young men, and here we sit and overlook this great scene, this accumulation, this wreckage of passion and splendour. (*More quietly*) It all brings back the past a little too acutely.
6. **Mrs Ansley:** Yes...yes...and reminds me of the future. We have to think of the future as well as the past. You know that Babs and I must return to New York soon, my dear, and if you'll just excuse me for just one moment I want to give the manager this cable to send for me. Just the confirmation of our passages home... better to confirm early than risk disappointment. (*Scrapes back chair and moves off*) Excuse me, I won't be a moment.
7. **Mrs Slade:** Certainly, take your time. (*Calls after her*) I'm perfectly happy here with the view.

(*Lower background under*)

8. **Mrs Slade:** (*Thinking aloud again*) Yes – the great problem with the past is that it raises the future... She'll be alright; she knows that her Babs will almost certainly come back to Rome engaged to that boy... she won't need those passages home but trust Grace to be secure just in case. He couldn't be much more eligible... and Grace will sell the New York house, and settle down near the Campolieris in Rome, but never be in their way... She'll have an excellent cook and

Jealous Love

1. **Mrs Slade (contd):** just the right people in for bridge and cocktails... and a perfectly peaceful old age among her grandchildren. Grace has always been so tactful – even in her emotions – she couldn't be affected by the memories that rise like ghosts from these ruins for me; there is nothing for Grace to remember, and nothing for her to worry about. Still... after all this time – why do I have to think so unkindly about Grace Ansley? She's done nothing to deserve it... perhaps after all it is envy. As a girl she always seemed so tranquil... hers was a quiet beauty and her charm stole up on you unawares. Yes, it was the subtlety of Grace's attractions that frightened me so much during that winter in Rome when Delphin and I had just become engaged to be married... Somehow the figure of Grace interposes itself between me and my memories of our engagement... There's something in the atmosphere now that brings that time back in a strange and vivid way. Perhaps it's just the fact of running into Grace Ansley after all these years of perfunctory New York greetings at Christmas and brief exchanges of condolence at widowhood... and here in Rome of all places.

(Bring up background)

2. **Mrs Ansley:** *(Approaching)* Well, that's done. *(FX sits)*
3. **Mrs Slade:** Yes...good...*(Abruptly)* The sun's set... you're not afraid my dear?
4. **Mrs Ansley:** *(Slightly startled)* Afraid?
5. **Mrs Slade:** Of Roman Fever, of pneumonia? I remember how ill you were that winter. You had a very delicate throat as a girl didn't you?
6. **Mrs Ansley:** Oh, we're alright up here; down below, in the Forum, it does get deathly cold, all of a sudden... but not up here.
7. **Mrs Slade:** Of course you know because you had to be so careful. *(Making an effort to soften her tone)* Whenever I look at the Forum from up here I remember that story about a great-aunt of yours... wasn't she? A dreadfully wicked great-aunt.

Roman Fever

1. **Mrs Ansley:** (*With a slight laugh*) Oh, yes, great-aunt Harriet. She was the one who was supposed to have sent her young sister out to the Forum after sunset to gather a night-blooming flower for her album. All our great-aunts and grandmothers used to have albums of dried flowers, you know.
2. **Mrs Slade:** Yes. But didn't she really send her there because they were in love with the same man?
3. **Mrs Ansley:** Well, so family tradition would have it. They say Aunt Harriet confessed it years afterwards. At any rate her poor little sister caught the fever and died. Mother used to frighten us with the story when we were children.
4. **Mrs Slade:** And you frightened me with it in turn... that winter you and I were here as girls. That winter I was engaged to Delphin.
5. **Mrs Ansley:** Did I really?... Frighten you?... I can't believe that you were easily frightened.
6. **Mrs Slade:** No, I'm not; not often. But I was then. I was easily frightened because I was too happy. I wonder if you can imagine what that means?
7. **Mrs Ansley:** I... well... yes.
8. **Mrs Slade:** (*Determinedly*) I suppose that was why the story of your wicked aunt made such an impression on me. And I thought: 'There's no such thing as Roman Fever any more, but the Forum is desperately cold after sunset – especially after a hot day. And the Colosseum's even colder and damper.
9. **Mrs Ansley:** The Colosseum?
10. **Mrs Slade:** Yes. The Colosseum. (*A little hysterically*) It wasn't easy to get in there, you know... after the gates were locked for the night. Far from easy. Still in those days it could be managed... anything could... and it was managed...often. Lovers met there who couldn't meet elsewhere. Did you know that?
11. **Mrs Ansley:** I – I daresay. I don't remember.
12. **Mrs Slade:** Don't you remember? Don't you remember going to visit some ruins or other one evening, just after

Jealous Love

1. **Mrs Slade (contd):** dark, and catching a bad chill? We heard that you were supposed to have gone to see the moon rise. People always said that that expedition was what caused your illness.
2. **Mrs Ansley:** Did they?... It was all so long ago.
3. **Mrs Slade:** Yes. And you did get well again... so it didn't matter after all... But I suppose it struck your friends as strange – the reason for your illness, I mean... we all knew how prudent you always were on account of your throat and how your mother always took such care of you... You had been out sightseeing late, hadn't you, that night?...
4. **Mrs Ansley:** Perhaps I had. The most prudent girls aren't always so prudent, you know. What made you think of it now?
5. **Mrs Slade:** (*Suddenly, after a short pause*) Because I simply can't bear it any longer!
6. **Mrs Ansley:** (*Catching her breath*) Can't bear what?
7. **Mrs Slade:** Why – your ignorance of the fact that I've always known why you went.
8. **Mrs Ansley:** Why I went?
9. **Mrs Slade:** Yes. You think I'm bluffing, don't you? Well, I'm not. You went to meet the man I was engaged to... and I can repeat every word of the letter that took you there.

(*Gasp and noise of Mrs Ansley's bag, gloves, knitting, etc. falling to the floor and her chair scraping slightly as she stands up*)

10. **Mrs Ansley:** No, no. Please don't go on.
11. **Mrs Slade:** Why not? Listen – this will convince you. 'My one darling, things can't go on like this. I must see you alone. Come to the Colosseum immediately after dark tomorrow. There will be somebody to let you in. No one whom you need fear will suspect.' – but perhaps you'd forgotten what the letter said?
12. **Mrs Ansley:** (*Steadying her voice*) No. I know it by heart too.
13. **Mrs Slade:** And the signature? 'Only your D.S.' (*Rising voice*) Was that it? I'm right, am I? That was the letter that

Roman Fever

1. **Mrs Slade (contd):** made you less 'prudent'?... that made you go out that evening after dark?
2. **Mrs Ansley:** (*Short pause as she sits*) I don't know how you knew. I burnt that letter at once.
3. **Mrs Slade:** Yes, you would naturally. You're so 'prudent' after all! And if you're wondering how on earth I know what was in it since you burnt it...That's it, isn't it?... (*Pause but no reply*) Well, my dear, I know what was in that letter because I wrote it.
4. **Mrs Ansley:** You wrote it?
5. **Mrs Slade:** Yes,
6. **Mrs Ansley:** Oh... (*Tearfully*) It was the only letter I ever had from him and you say you wrote it.
7. **Mrs Slade:** Yes, I wrote it! But I was the girl he was engaged to. Did you happen to remember that?
8. **Mrs Ansley:** I'm not trying to excuse myself... I remembered... I knew...
9. **Mrs Slade:** And still you went?
10. **Mrs Ansley:** Still I went.
11. **Mrs Slade:** (*With some small compunction in her voice now*) You do understand? I'd found out... and I hated you... hated you. I knew you were in love with Delphin – and I was afraid; afraid of you, of your quiet ways, your sweetness... your... Well, I wanted you out of the way, that's all. Just for a few weeks; just till I was sure of him... So, in a blind fury I wrote that letter... I don't know why I'm telling you now.
12. **Mrs Ansley:** (*Slowly*) I suppose it's because you've always gone on hating me.
13. **Mrs Slade:** Perhaps that's it... or perhaps I just wanted to get the whole thing off my mind. Being here...with you... looking down on the city like this; it brings it all back so powerfully... I'm glad you destroyed the letter. Of course I never thought you'd nearly die. (*Pause*) I suppose you think me a monster.
14. **Mrs Ansley:** I don't know... I wasn't thinking of you... it was the only letter I had and now you say he didn't write it.
15. **Mrs Slade:** How you care for him still!

45

1. **Mrs Ansley:** I cared for that memory.

(*The noise of the restaurant becomes slightly more noticeable again*)

2. **Mrs Slade:** You did your best to get him away from me, didn't you? But you failed; I kept him. That's all there is to say, isn't it?
3. **Mrs Ansley:** Yes, that's all.
4. **Mrs Slade:** I wish now I hadn't told you. I'd no idea you'd feel like this about it... that it could possibly mean so much to you. I thought you'd be amused. It all happened so long ago, as you say... you must do me the justice to remember that I had no reason to believe that you'd ever taken it seriously. (*With a laugh*) How could I, when you were married to Horace Ansley two months afterwards? As soon as you could get out of bed your mother rushed you off to Florence and married you. People were rather surprised... they wondered why it was done so quickly; but I knew why. I had an idea that you did it out of spite... To be able to say that you'd got ahead of Delphin and me you married Horace Ansley. Girls have such silly reasons for doing the most important things... Well... your marrying so soon convinced me that you'd never really cared.
5. **Mrs Ansley:** (*Self-possessed now*) Yes, I suppose it would.

(*Silence falls between the two ladies whilst a mild commotion between a waiter and a lady with an English voice becomes apparent*)

6. **English Lady:** (*Off*) I know I dropped it here... it's so dark now I can't see properly... Would you put on the terrace lights please?
7. **Waiter:** (*Also off*) Of course, Madame.
8. **English Lady:** (*Approaching*) I don't suppose either of you ladies happened to notice where I dropped my elastic band, did you?
9. **Mrs Slade** } No... no... sorry.
   Mrs Ansley
10. **English Lady:** Such a nuisance; my Baedeker will fall entirely to pieces if I don't hold it together with something.

Roman Fever

1. **English Lady (contd):** No point in going anywhere without one's guidebook, is there? Though I don't suppose those jolly girls you had with you earlier do much looking in books on their travels. The tall, jolly one is your daughter is she?
2. **Mrs Slade:** No; my daughter Jenny is the slighter girl of the two. Barbara is the daughter of my friend here.
3. **English Lady:** Oh yes, either way, jolly girls the pair of them. Nothing to compare with your young Americans abroad. So free and active, trampling on convention and frightening us Europeans out of our stodgy old ways. Ah! (*Bends down*) Here we are, my elastic! Well, very nice to have met you... (*Moving off slowly*) I hope you and your daughters enjoy the rest of your stay in Rome.

(*Pause as background noise heightens the brief silence between the two*)

4. **Mrs Slade:** I suppose I sent the letter as a kind of joke...
5. **Mrs Ansley:** (*Querying yet aghast*) A joke –?
6. **Mrs Slade:** Well, girls are ferocious at times, you know. Girls in love especially. I remember laughing to myself all through that evening at the idea that you were waiting around there, that huge and echoing ruin... all in darkness... dodging out of sight... listening for every sound, trying to get in... Of course, I was upset later when I heard you were so ill after that night.
7. **Mrs Ansley:** But I didn't have to wait. He'd arranged everything. He was there and we were let in at once.
8. **Mrs Slade:** (*Violently*) Delphin there? They let you in? Ah, now I know you're lying!
9. **Mrs Ansley:** (*Clearly with just a hint of surprise*) But of course he was there. Naturally he came to meet me.
10. **Mrs Slade:** Came? How could he have come? How could he have known he'd find you there? You must be raving!
11. **Mrs Ansley:** (*Hesitating*) But I answered the letter. I told him that I would be there. And he came to meet me.

Jealous Love

1. **Mrs Slade:** Oh God... you answered? I never once thought of you answering....
2. **Mrs Ansley:** It's odd you never thought of an answer if you wrote the letter.
3. **Mrs Slade:** (*Painfully*) I told you... I was blind with rage.
4. **Mrs Ansley:** It is cold here. (*FX Gets up*) We'd better go. I'm very sorry for you.
5. **Mrs Slade:** (*Dully*) Yes, we'd better go now... I don't know why you should feel sorry for me.
6. **Mrs Ansley:** Well...because I didn't have to wait that night... over there... in the Colosseum.
7. **Mrs Slade:** (*With a bitter laugh*) Yes, you beat me there. But I suppose I shouldn't begrudge it to you... After all these years. I had everything... I must remember that. I had him for twenty-five years (*Beginning to move off slowly*) and you had nothing but the memory of that one letter he didn't even write.

(*Pause for footsteps to cease*)

8. **Mrs Ansley:** I had Barbara.

(*Music*)

The Demon Lover

Elizabeth Bowen

Towards the end of her day in London Mrs Drover went round to her shut-up house to look for several things she wanted to take away. Some belonged to herself, some to her family, who were by now used to their country life. It was late August; it had been a steamy, showery day: at the moment the trees down the pavement glittered in an escape of humid yellow afternoon sun. Against the next batch of clouds, already piling up ink-dark, broken chimneys and parapets stood out. In her once familiar street, as in any unused channel, an unfamiliar queerness had silted up; a cat wove itself in and out of the railings, but no human eye watched Mrs Drover's return. Shifting some parcels under her arm, she slowly forced round her latchkey in an unwilling lock, then gave the door, which had warped, a push with her knee. Dead air came out to meet her as she went in.

The staircase window having been boarded up, no light came down into the hall. But one door, she could just see, stood ajar, so she went quickly through into the room and unshuttered the big window in there. Now the prosaic woman, looking about her, was more perplexed than she knew by everything that she saw, by traces of her long former habit of life – the yellow smoke-stain up the white marble mantlepiece, the ring left by a vase on the top of the escritoire; the bruise in the wallpaper where, on the door being thrown open widely, the china handle had always hit the wall. The piano, having gone away to be stored, had left what looked like claw-marks on its part of the parquet. Though not much dust had seeped in, each object wore a film of another kind; and, the only ventilation being the chimney, the whole drawing-room smelled of the cold hearth. Mrs Drover put down her parcels on the escritoire and left the room to proceed upstairs; the things she wanted were in a bedroom chest.

She had been anxious to see how the house was – the part-time caretaker she shared with some neighbours was away this week on his holiday, known to be not yet back. At the best of times he did not look in often, and she was never sure that she trusted him. There were some cracks in the structure, left by the last bombing, on which she was anxious to keep an eye. Not that one could do anything –

A shaft of refracted daylight now lay across the hall. She stopped dead and stared at the hall table – on this lay a letter addressed to her.

She thought first – then the caretaker *must* be back. All the same, who, seeing the house shuttered, would have dropped a letter in at the box? It was not a circular, it was not a bill. And the post office redirected, to the address in the country, everything for her that came through the post. The caretaker (even if he *were* back) did not know she was due in London today – her call here had been planned to be a surprise – so his negligence in the manner of this letter, leaving it to wait in the dusk and the dust, annoyed her. Annoyed, she picked up the letter, which bore no stamp. But it cannot be important, or they would know... She took the letter rapidly upstairs with her, without a stop to look at the writing till she reached what had been her bedroom, where she let in light. The room looked over the garden and other gardens: the sun had gone in; as the clouds sharpened and lowered, the trees and rank lawns seemed already to smoke with dark. Her reluctance to look again at the letter came from the fact that she felt intruded upon – and by someone contemptuous of her ways. However, in the tenseness preceding the fall of rain she read it: it was a few lines.

> Dear Kathleen: You will not have forgotten that today is our anniversary, and the day we said. The years have gone by at once slowly and fast. In view of the fact that nothing has changed, I shall rely upon you to keep your promise. I was sorry to see you leave London, but was satisfied that you would be back in time. You may expect me, therefore, at the hour arranged. Until then... K.

The Demon Lover

Mrs Drover looked for the date: it was today's. She dropped the letter on to the bed-springs, then picked it up to see the writing again – her lips, beneath the remains of lipstick, beginning to go white. She felt so much the change in her own face that she went to the mirror, polished a clear patch in it and looked at once urgently and stealthily in. She was confronted by a woman of forty-four, with eyes starting out under a hat-brim that had been rather carelessly pulled down. She had not put on any more powder since she left the shop where she ate her solitary tea. The pearls her husband had given her on their marriage hung loose round her now rather thinner throat, slipping in the V of the pink wool jumper her sister knitted last autumn as they sat round the fire. Mrs Drover's most normal expression was one of controlled worry, but of assent. Since the birth of the third of her little boys, attended by a quite serious illness, she had had an intermittent muscular flicker to the left of her mouth, but in spite of this she could always sustain a manner that was at once energetic and calm.

Turning from her own face as precipitately as she had gone to meet it, she went to the chest where the things were, unlocked it, threw up the lid and knelt to search. But as rain began to come crashing down she could not keep from looking over her shoulder at the stripped bed on which the letter lay. Behind the blanket of rain the clock of the church that still stood struck six – with rapidly heightening apprehension she counted each of the slow strokes. 'The hour arranged... My God,' she said, '*what hour? How should I...? After twenty-five years...*'

The young girl talking to the soldier in the garden had not ever completely seen his face. It was dark; they were saying goodbye under a tree. Now and then – for it felt, from not seeing him at this intense moment, as though she had never seen him at all – she verified his presence for these few moments longer by putting out a hand, which he each time pressed, without very much kindness, and painfully, on to one of the breast buttons of his uniform. That cut of the button on the palm of her hand was, principally what she was to carry away. This was so near the end of a leave from France that she could only wish him already gone. It was August 1916. Being not kissed, being drawn away from and looked at intimidated Kathleen till she imagined spectral glitters in the place of his eyes. Turning away and looking back up the lawn she saw, through branches of trees, the drawing-room window alight: she caught a breath for the moment when she could go running back there into the safe arms of her mother and sister, and cry: 'What shall I do, what shall I do? He has gone.'

Hearing her catch her breath, her fiancé said, without feeling: 'Cold?'

'You're going away such a long way.'

'Not so far as you think.'

'I don't understand?'

'You don't have to,' he said. 'You will. You know what we said.'

'But that was – suppose you – I mean, suppose.'

'I shall be with you,' he said, 'sooner or later. You won't forget that. You need do nothing but wait.'

Only a little more than a minute later she was free to run up the silent lawn. Looking in through the window at her mother and sister, who did not for the moment perceive her, she already felt that unnatural promise drive down between her and the rest of all human kind. No other way of having given herself could have made her feel so apart, lost and foresworn. She could not have plighted a more sinister troth.

Kathleen behaved well when, some months later, her fiancé was reported missing, presumed killed. Her family not only supported her but were able to praise her courage without stint because they could not regret, as a husband for her, the man they knew almost nothing about. They hoped she would, in a year or two, console herself – and had it been only a question of consolation things might have gone much straighter ahead. But her trouble, behind just a little grief, was a complete dislocation from everything. She did not reject other lovers, for these failed to appear: for years she failed to attract men – and with the approach of her 'thirties she became natural enough to share her family's anxiousness on this score. She began to put herself out, to wonder; and at thirty-two she was very greatly relieved to find herself being courted by William Drover. She married him, and the two of them settled down in this quiet, arboreal part of Kensington: in this house the years piled up, her children were born and they all lived till they were driven out by the bombs of the next war. Her movements as Mrs Drover were circumscribed, and she dismissed any idea that they were still watched.

As things were – dead or living the letter-writer sent her only a threat. Unable, for some minutes, to go on kneeling with her back exposed to the empty room, Mrs Drover rose from the chest to sit on an upright chair whose back was firmly against the wall. The desuetude of her former bedroom, her married London home's whole air of being a cracked cup from which memory, with its reassuring power, had either evaporated or leaked away, made a crisis – and at just this crisis the letter-writer had, knowledgeably, struck. The hollowness of the house this evening cancelled years on years of voices, habits and steps. Through the shut windows she only heard rain fall on the roofs around. To rally herself, she said she was in a mood – and for two or three seconds shutting her eyes told herself that she had imagined the letter. But she opened them – there it lay on the bed.

On the supernatural side of the letter's entrance she was not permitting her mind to dwell. Who, in London, knew she meant to call at the house today? Evidently, however, this had been known. The caretaker, *had* he come back, had had no cause to expect her: he would have taken the letter in his pocket, to forward it, at his own time, through the post. There was no other sign that the caretaker had been in – but, if not? Letters dropped in at doors of deserted houses do not fly or walk to tables in halls. They do not sit on the dust of empty tables with an air of certainty that they will be found. There is needed some human hand – but nobody but the caretaker had a key. Under circumstances she did not care to consider, a house can be entered without a key. It was possible that she was not alone now. She might be being waited for, downstairs. Waited for – until when? Until 'the hour arranged'. At least that was not six o'clock: six has struck.

She rose from the chair and went over and locked the door.

The thing was, to get out. To fly? No, not that: she had to catch her train. As a woman whose utter dependability was the keystone of her family life she was not willing to return to the country, to her husband, her little boys and her sister, without the objects she had come up to fetch. Resuming work at the chest she set about making up a number of parcels in a rapid, fumbling-decisive way. These, with her shopping parcels, would be too much to carry; these meant a taxi – at the thought of the taxi her heart went up and her normal breathing resumed. I will ring up the taxi now; the taxi cannot come too soon: I shall hear the taxi out there running its engine, till I walk calmly down to it through the hall. I'll ring up – But no: the telephone is cut off... She tugged at a knot she had tied wrong.

The idea of flight... He was never kind to me, not really. I don't remember him kind at all. Mother said he never considered me. He was set on me, that was what it was – not love. Not love, not meaning a person well. What did he do, to make me promise like that? I can't remember – But she found that she could.

She remembered with such dreadful acuteness that the twenty-five years since then dissolved like smoke and she instinctively looked for the weal left by the button on the palm of her hand. She remembered not only all that he said and did but the complete suspension of *her* existence during that August week. I was not myself – they all told me so at the time. She remembered – but with one white burning blank as where acid has dropped on a photograph: *under no conditions* could she remember his face.

So, wherever he may be waiting, I shall not know him. You have no time to run from a face you do not expect.

The thing was to get to the taxi before any clock struck what could be the hour. She would slip down the street and round the side of the square to where the square gave on the main road.

The Demon Lover

She would return in the taxi, safe, to her own door, and bring the solid driver into the house with her to pick up the parcels from room to room. The idea of that taxi driver made her decisive, bold: she unlocked her door, went to the top of the staircase and listened down.

She heard nothing – but while she was hearing nothing the *passé* air of the staircase was disturbed by a draught that travelled up to her face. It emanated from the basement: down there a door or window was being opened by someone who chose this moment to leave the house.

The rain had stopped; the pavements steamily shone as Mrs Drover let herself out by inches from her own front door into the empty street. The unoccupied houses opposite continued to meet her look with their damaged stare. Making towards the thorough-fare and the taxi, she tried not to keep looking behind. Indeed, the silence was so intense – one of those creeks of London silence exaggerated this summer by the damage of war – that no tread could have gained on hers unheard. Where her street debouched on the square where people went on living, she grew conscious of, and checked, her unnatural pace. Across the open end of the square two buses impassively passed each other: women, a perambulator, cyclists, a man wheeling a barrow signalized, once again, the ordinary flow of life. At the square's most populous corner should be – and was – the short taxi rank. This evening, only one taxi – but this, although it presented its blank rump, appeared already to be alertly waiting for her. Indeed, without looking round the driver started his engine as she panted up from behind and put her hand on the door. As she did so, the clock struck seven. The taxi faced the main road: to make the trip back to her house it would have to turn – she had settled back on the seat and the taxi *had* turned before she, surprised by its knowing movement, recollected that she had not 'said where'. She leaned forward to scratch at the glass panel that divided the driver's head from her own.

The driver braked to what was almost a stop, turned around and slid the glass panel back: the jolt of this flung Mrs Drover forward till her face was almost into the glass. Through the aperture driver and passenger, not six inches between them, remained for an eternity eye to eye. Mrs Drover's mouth hung open for some seconds before she could issue her first scream. After that she continued to scream freely and to beat with her gloved hands on the glass all round as the taxi, accelerating without mercy, made off with her into the hinterland of deserted streets.

An Attempt at Jealousy

Craig Raine

So how is life with your new bloke?
Simpler, I bet. Just one stroke
of his quivering oar and the skin
of the Thames goes into a spin,

eh? How is life with an oarsman? Better?
More in–out? Athletic? Wetter?
When you hear the moan of the rowlocks,
do you urge him on like a cox?

Tell me, is he bright enough to find
that memo-pad you call a mind?
Or has he contrived to bring you out –
given you an in-tray and an out?

How did I ever fall for a paper-clip?
How could I ever listen to office gossip
even in bed and find it so intelligent?
Was it straight biological bent?

I suppose you go jogging together?
Tackle the Ridgeway in nasty weather?
Face force 5 gales and chat about prep
or how you bested that Birmingham rep?

He must be mad with excitement.
So must you. What an incitement
to lust all those press-ups must be.
Or is it just the same? PE?

Jealous Love

Tell me, I'm curious. Is it fun
being in love with just anyone?
How do you remember his face
if you meet in a public place?

Perhaps you know him by his shoes?
Or do you sometimes choose
another pinstriped clone
by accident and drag that home

instead? From what you say,
he's perfect. For a Chekhov play.
Tall and dark and brightly dim,
Kulygin's part was made for him.

Imagine your life with a 'beak'.
Week after week after week
like homework or detention;
all that standing to attention

whenever his colleagues drop in
for a spot of what's-your-toxin.
Speech Day, matron, tuck-shop, Christ,
you'll find school fees are over-priced

and leave, but not come back to me.
You've done your bit for poetry.
Words, or deeds? You'll stick to youth.
I'm a stickler for the truth –

which makes me wonder what it was
I loved you for. Tell me, because
now I feel nothing – except regret.
What is it, love, I need to forget?

Song: Go, and Catch a Falling Star

John Donne

Go, and catch a falling star,
   Get with child a mandrake root,
Tell me, where all past years are,
   Or who cleft the Devil's foot,
Teach me to hear mermaids singing,
   Or to keep off envy's stinging,
       And find
       What wind
Serves to advance an honest mind.

If thou be'est born to strange sights,
   Things invisible to see,
Ride ten thousand days and nights,
   Till age snow white hairs on thee,
Thou, when thou return'st, wilt tell me
All strange wonders that befell thee,
       And swear
       No where
Lives a woman true, and fair.

If thou find'st one, let me know,
   Such a pilgrimage were sweet,
Yet do not, I would not go,
   Though at next door we might meet,
Though she were true, when you met her,
And last, till you write your letter,
       Yet she
       Will be
False, ere I come, to two, or three.

Loving the Family...
and Other Animals
A Domestic Dilemma

Carson McCullers

On Thursday Martin Meadows left the office early enough to make the first express bus home. It was the hour when the evening lilac glow was fading in the slushy streets, but by the time the bus had left the Mid-town terminal the bright city night had come. On Thursdays the maid had a half-day off and Martin liked to get home as soon as possible, since for the past year his wife had not been – well. This Thursday he was very tired and, hoping that no regular commuter would single him out for conversation, he fastened his attention to the newspaper until the bus had crossed the George Washington Bridge. Once on 9–W Highway Martin always felt that the trip was halfway done, he breathed deeply, even in cold weather when only ribbons of draught cut through the smoky air of the bus, confident that he was breathing country air. It used to be that at this point he would relax and begin to think with pleasure of his home. But in this last year nearness brought only a sense of tension and he did not anticipate the journey's end. This evening Martin kept his face close to the window and watched the barren fields and lonely lights of passing townships. There was a moon, pale on the dark earth and areas of late, porous snow; to Martin the countryside seemed vast and somehow desolate that evening. He took his hat from the rack and put his folded newspaper in the pocket of his overcoat a few minutes before time to pull the cord.

The cottage was a block from the bus stop, near the river but not directly on the shore; from the living-room window you

A Domestic Dilemma

could look across the street and opposite yard and see the Hudson. The cottage was modern, almost too white and new on the narrow plot of yard. In summer the grass was soft and bright and Martin carefully tended a flower border and a rose trellis. But during the cold, fallow months the yard was bleak and the cottage seemed naked. Lights were on that evening in all the rooms in the little house and Martin hurried up the front walk. Before the steps he stopped to move a wagon out of the way.

The children were in the living room, so intent on play that the opening of the front door was at first unnoticed. Martin stood looking at his safe, lovely children. They had opened the bottom drawer of the secretary and taken out the Christmas decorations. Andy had managed to plug in the Christmas tree lights and the green and red bulbs glowed with out-of-season festivity on the rug of the living room. At the moment he was trying to trail the bright cord over Marianne's rocking horse. Marianne sat on the floor pulling off an angel's wings. The children wailed a startling welcome. Martin swung the fat little baby girl up to his shoulder and Andy threw himself against his father's legs.

'Daddy, Daddy, Daddy!'

Martin sat down the little girl carefully and swung Andy a few times like a pendulum. Then he picked up the Christmas tree cord.

'What's all this stuff doing out? Help me put it back in the drawer. You're not to fool with the light socket. Remember I told you that before. I mean it, Andy.'

The six-year-old child nodded and shut the secretary drawer. Martin stroked his fair soft hair and his hand lingered tenderly on the nape of the child's frail neck.

'Had supper yet, Bumpkin?'

'It hurt. The toast was hot.'

The baby girl stumbled on the rug and, after the first surprise of the fall, began to cry; Martin picked her up and carried her in his arms back to the kitchen.

'See, Daddy,' said Andy. 'The toast—'

Emily had laid the children's supper on the uncovered porcelain table. There were two plates with the remains of cream-of-wheat and eggs and silver mugs that had held milk. There was also a platter of cinnamon toast, untouched, except for one tooth-marked bite. Martin sniffed the bitten piece and nibbled gingerly. Then he put the toast into the garbage pail.

'Hoo – phui – What on earth!'

Emily had mistaken the tin of cayenne for the cinnamon.

'I like to have burnt up,' Andy said. 'Drank water and ran outdoors and opened my mouth. Marianne didn't eat none.'

'Any,' corrected Martin. He stood helpless, looking around the walls of the kitchen. 'Well, that's that, I guess,' he said finally. 'Where is your mother now?'

'She's up in you alls' room.'

Martin left the children in the kitchen and went up to his wife. Outside the door he waited for a moment to still his anger. He did not knock and once inside the room he closed the door behind him.

Emily sat in the rocking chair by the window of the pleasant room. She had been drinking something from a tumbler and as he entered she put the glass hurriedly on the floor behind the chair. In her attitude there was confusion and guilt which she tried to hide by a show of spurious vivacity.

'Oh, Marty! You home already? The time slipped up on me. I was just going down —' She lurched to him and her kiss was strong with sherry. When he stood unresponsive she stepped back a pace and giggled nervously.

'What's the matter with you? Standing there like a barber pole. Is anything wrong with you?'

'Wrong with *me*?' Martin bent over the rocking chair and picked up the tumbler from the floor. 'If you could only realize how sick I am – how bad it is for all of us.'

Emily spoke in a false, airy voice that had become too familiar to him. Often at such times she affected a slight English accent copying perhaps some actress she admired. 'I haven't the vaguest idea what you mean. Unless you are referring to the glass I used for a spot of sherry. I had a finger of sherry – maybe two. But what is the crime in that, pray tell me? I'm quite all right. Quite all right.'

'So anyone can see.'

As she went into the bathroom Emily walked with careful gravity. She turned on the cold water and dashed some on her face with her cupped hands, then patted herself dry with the corner of a bath towel. Her face was delicately featured and young, unblemished.

'I was just going down to make dinner.' She tottered and balanced herself by holding to the door frame.

'I'll take care of dinner. You stay up here. I'll bring it up.'

'I'll do nothing of the sort. Why, whoever heard of such a thing?'

'Please,' Martin said.

'Leave me alone. I'm quite all right. I was just on the way down —'

'Mind what I say.'

'Mind your grandmother.'

She lurched toward the door, but Martin caught her by the arm. 'I don't want the children to see you in this condition. Be reasonable.'

'Condition!' Emily jerked her arm. Her voice rose angrily. 'Why, because I drink a couple of sherries in the afternoon you're trying to make me out a drunkard. Condition! Why, I don't even touch whiskey. As well you know. *I* don't swill liquor at bars. And that's more than you can say. I don't even have a cocktail at dinnertime. I only sometimes have a glass of sherry. What, I ask you, is the disgrace of that? Condition!'

Martin sought words to calm his wife. 'We'll have a quiet supper by ourselves up here. That's a good girl.' Emily sat on the side of the bed and he opened the door for a quick departure.

'I'll be back in a jiffy.'

As he busied himself with the dinner downstairs he was lost in the familiar question as to how this problem had come upon his home. He himself had always enjoyed a good drink. When they were still living in Alabama they had served long drinks or cocktails as a matter of course. For years they had drunk one or two – possibly three drinks before dinner, and at bedtime a long nightcap. Evenings before holidays they might get a buzz on, might even become a little tight. But alcohol had never seemed a problem to him, only a bothersome expense that with the increase in the family they could scarcely afford. It was only after his company had transferred him to New York that Martin was aware that certainly his wife was drinking too much. She was tippling, he noticed, during the day.

The problem acknowledged, he tried to analyse the source. The change from Alabama to New York had somehow disturbed her; accustomed to the idle warmth of a small Southern town, the matrix of the family and cousinship and childhood friends, she had failed to accommodate herself to the stricter, lonelier mores of the North. The duties of motherhood and housekeeping were onerous to her. Homesick for Paris City, she had made no friends in the suburban town. She read only magazines and murder books. Her interior life was insufficient without the artifice of alcohol.

The revelations of incontinence insidiously undermined his previous conceptions of his wife. There were times of unexplainable malevolence, times when the alcoholic fuse caused an explosion of unseemly anger. He encountered a latent coarseness in Emily, inconsistent with her natural simplicity. She lied about drinking and deceived him with unsuspected stratagems.

Then there was an accident. Coming home from work one evening about a year ago, he was greeted with screams from the children's room. He found Emily holding the baby, wet and naked from her bath. The baby had been dropped, her frail, frail skull striking the table edge, so that a thread of blood was soaking into the gossamer hair. Emily was sobbing and intoxicated. As Martin cradled the hurt child, so infinitely precious at the moment, he had an affrighted vision of the future.

The next day Marianne was all right. Emily vowed that never again would she touch liquor, and for a few weeks she was sober, cold and downcast. Then gradually she began – not whiskey or gin – but quantities of beer, or sherry, or outlandish liqueurs; once he had come across a hatbox of empty crème de menthe bottles. Martin found a dependable maid who managed the household competently. Virgie was also from Alabama and Martin had never dared tell Emily the wage scale customary in New York. Emily's drinking was entirely secret now, done before he reached the house. Usually the effects were almost imperceptible – a looseness of movement or the heavy-lidded eyes. The time of irresponsibilities, such as the cayenne-pepper toast were rare, and Martin could dismiss his worries when Virgie was at the house. But, nevertheless, anxiety was always latent, a threat of undefined disaster that underlaid his days.

'Marianne!' Martin called, for even the recollection of that time brought the need for reassurance. The baby girl, no longer hurt, but no less precious to her father, came into the kitchen with her brother. Martin went on with the preparations for the meal. He opened a can of soup and put two chops in the frying pan. Then he sat down by the table and took Marianne on his knees for a pony ride. Andy watched them, his fingers wobbling the tooth that had been loose all that week.

'Andy-the-candyman!' Martin said. 'Is that old critter still in you mouth? Come closer, let Daddy have a look.'

'I got a string to pull it with.' The child brought from his pocket a tangled thread. 'Virgie said to tie it to the tooth and tie the other end to the doorknob and shut the door real suddenly.'

Martin took out a clean handkerchief and felt the loose tooth carefully. 'That tooth is coming out of my Andy's mouth tonight. Otherwise I'm awfully afraid we'll have a tooth tree in the family.'

'A what?'

'A tooth tree,' Martin said. 'You'll bite into something and swallow that tooth. And the tooth will take root in poor Andy's stomach and grow into a tooth tree with sharp little teeth instead of leaves.'

'Shoo, Daddy,' Andy said. But he held the tooth firmly between his grimy little thumb and forefinger. 'There ain't any tree like that. I never seen one.'

'There *isn't* any trees like that and I never *saw* one.'

Martin tensed suddenly. Emily was coming down the stairs. He listended to her fumbling footsteps, his arm embracing the little boy with dread. When Emily came into the room he saw from her movements and her sullen face that she had again been at the sherry bottle. She began to yank open drawers and set the table.

'Condition!' she said in a furry voice. 'You talk to me like that. Don't think I'll forget. I remember every dirty lie you say to me. Don't you think for a minute that I forget.'

'Emily!' he begged. 'The children —'

'The children – yes! Don't think I don't see through your dirty plots and schemes. Down here trying to turn my own children against me. Don't think I don't see and understand.'

'Emily! I beg you – please go upstairs.'

'So you can turn my children – my very own children –' Two large tears coursed rapidly down her cheeks. 'Trying to turn my little boy, my Andy, against his own mother.'

With drunken impulsiveness Emily knelt on the floor before the startled child. Her hands on his shoulders balanced her. 'Listen, my Andy – you wouldn't listen to any lies your father tells you? You wouldn't believe what he says? Listen, Andy, what was your father telling you before I came downstairs?' Uncertain, the child sought his father's face. 'Tell me. Mama wants to know.'

'About the tooth tree.'

'What?'

The child repeated the words and she echoed them with unbelieving terror. 'The tooth tree!' she swayed and renewed her grasp on the child's shoulder. 'I don't know what you're talking about. But listen, Andy, Mama is all right, isn't she?' The tears were spilling down her face and Andy drew back from her, for he was afraid. Grasping the table edge, Emily stood up.

'See! You have turned my child against me.'

Marianne began to cry, and Martin took her in his arms.

'That's all right, you can take *your* child. You have always shown partiality from the very first. I don't mind, but at least you can leave me my little boy.'

Andy edged close to his father and touched his leg. 'Daddy,' he wailed.

Martin took the children to the foot of the stairs. 'Andy, you take up Marianne and Daddy will follow you in a minute.'

'But Mama?' the child asked, whispering.

'Mama will be all right. Don't worry.'

Emily was sobbing at the kitchen table, her face buried in the crook of her arm. Martin poured a cup of soup and set it before her. Her rasping sobs unnerved him; the vehemence of her emotion, irrespective of the source, touched in him a strain of tenderness. Unwillingly he laid his hand on her dark hair. 'Sit up and drink the soup.' Her face as she looked up at him was chastened and imploring. The boy's withdrawal or the touch of Martin's hand had turned the tenor of her mood.

'Ma-Martin,' she sobbed. 'I'm so ashamed.'

'Drink the soup.'

Obeying him, she drank between the gasping breaths. After a second cup she allowed him to lead her up to their room. She was docile now and more restrained. He laid her nightgown on the bed and was about to leave the room when a fresh round of grief, the alcholic tumult, came again.

'He turned away. My Andy looked at me and turned away.'

Impatience and fatigue hardened his voice, but he spoke warily. 'You forget that Andy is still a little child – he can't comprehend the meaning of such scenes.'

'Did I make a scene? Oh Martin, did I make a scene before the children?'

Her horrified face touched and amused him against his will. 'Forget it. Put on your nightgown and go to sleep.'

'My child turned away from me. Andy looked at his mother and turned away. The children —'

She was caught in the rhythmic sorrow of alcohol. Martin withdrew from the room, saying: 'For God's sake go to sleep. The children will forget by tomorrow.'

As he said this he wondered if it were true. Would the scene glide so easily from memory – or would it root in the unconscious to fester in the after-years? Martin did not know, and the last alternative sickened him. He thought of Emily, foresaw the morning-after humiliation: the shards of memory, the lucidities that glared from the obliterating darkness of shame. She would call the New York office twice – possibly three or four times. Martin anticipated his own embarrassment, wondering if the others at the office could possibly suspect. He felt that his secretary had divined the trouble long ago and that she pitied him. He suffered a moment of rebellion against his fate, he hated his wife.

Once in the children's room he closed the door and felt secure for the first time that evening. Marianne fell down on the floor, picked herself up and calling: 'Daddy, watch me,' fell again, got up, and continued the falling-calling routine. Andy sat in the child's low chair, wobbling the tooth. Martin ran the water in the tub, washed his own hands in the lavatory, and called the boy into the bathroom.

'Let's have another look at that tooth.' Martin sat on the toilet, holding Andy between his knees. The child's mouth gaped and Martin grasped the tooth. A wobble, a quick twist and the nacreous milk tooth was free. Andy's face was for the first moment split between terror, astonishment, and delight. He mouthed a swallow of water, and spat into the lavatory.

'Look, Daddy! It's blood. Marianne!'

Martin loved to bathe his children, loved inexpressibly the tender, naked bodies as they stood in the water so exposed. It was not fair of Emily to say that he showed partiality. As Martin soaped the delicate boy-body of his son he felt that further love would be impossible. Yet he admitted the difference in the quality of his emotions for the two children. His love for his daughter was graver, touched with a strain of melancholy, a gentleness that was akin to pain. His pet names for the little boy were absurdities of daily inspiration – he called the little girl always Marianne, and his voice as he spoke it was a caress. Martin patted dry the fat baby stomach and the sweet little genital fold. The washed child faces were radiant as flower petals, equally loved.

'I'm putting the tooth under my pillow. I'm supposed to get a quarter.'

'What for?'

'*You* know, Daddy. Johnny got a quarter for his tooth.'

'Who puts the quarter there?' asked Martin. 'I used to think the fairies left it in the night. It was a dime in my day, though.'

'That's what they say in kindergarten.'

'Who does put it there?'

'Your parents,' Andy said. 'You!'

Martin was pinning the cover on Marianne's bed. His daughter was already asleep. Scarcely breathing, Martin bent over and kissed her forehead, kissed again the tiny hand that lay palm-upward, flung in slumber beside her head.

'Good night, Andy-man.'

The answer was only a drowsy murmur. After a minute Martin took out his change and slid a quarter underneath the pillow. He left a night light in the room.

As Martin prowled about the kitchen making a late meal, it occurred to him that the children had not once mentioned their mother or the scene that must have seemed to them incomprehensible. Absorbed in the instant – the tooth, the bath, the quarter – the fluid passage of child-time had borne these weightless episodes like leaves in the swift current of a shallow stream while the adult enigma was beached and forgotten on the shore. Martin thanked the Lord for that.

But his own anger, repressed and lurking, rose again. His youth was being frittered by a drunkard's waste, his very manhood subtly undermined. And the children, once the immunity of incomprehension passes – what would it be like in a year or so? With his elbows on the table he ate his food brutishly, untasting. There was no hiding the truth – soon there would be gossip in the office and in the town; his wife was a dissolute woman. Dissolute. And he and his children were bound to a future of degradation and slow ruin.

Martin pushed away from the table and stalked into the living room. He followed the lines of a book with his eyes but his mind conjured miserable images: he saw his children drowned in the river, his wife a disgrace on the public street. By bedtime the dull, hard anger was like a weight upon his chest and his feet dragged as he climbed the stairs.

The room was dark except for the shafting light from the half-opened bathroom door. Martin undressed quietly. Little by little, mysteriously, there came in him a change. His wife was asleep, her peaceful respiration sounding gentle in the room. Her high-heeled shoes with the carelessly dropped stockings made to him a mute appeal. Her underclothes were flung in disorder on the chair. Martin picked up the girdle and the soft, silk brassière and stood for a moment with them in his hands. For the first time that evening he looked at his wife. His eyes rested on the sweet forehead, the arch of the fine brow. The brow had descended to Marianne, and the tilt at the end of the delicate nose. In his son he could trace the high cheekbones and pointed chin. Her body was full-bosomed, slender and undulant. As Martin watched the tranquil slumber of his wife the ghost of the old anger vanished. All thoughts of blame or blemish were distant from him now. Martin put out the bathroom light and raised the window. Careful not to awaken Emily he slid into bed. By moonlight he watched his wife for the last time. His hand sought the adjacent flesh and sorrow paralleled desire in the immense complexity of love.

Arrangements

Douglas Dunn

'Is this the door?' This must be it. No, no.
We come across crowds and confetti, weddings
With well-wishers, relatives, whimsical bridesmaids.
Some have happened. Others are waiting their turn.
One is taking place before the Registrar.
A young groom is unsteady in his new shoes.
His bride is nervous on the edge of the future.
I walk through them with the father of my dead wife.
I redefine the meaning of 'strangers'.
Death, too, must have looked in on our wedding.
The building stinks of municipal function.
'Go through with it. You have to. It's the law.'
So I say to a clerk, 'I have come about a death.'
'In there,' she says. 'You came in by the wrong door.'

A woman with teenage children sits at a table.
She hands to the clerk the paper her doctor gave her.
'Does that mean 'heart attack'? she asks.
How little she knows, this widow. Or any of us.
From one look she can tell I have not come
With my uncle, on the business of my aunt.
A flake of confetti falls from her fur shoulder.
There is a bond between us, a terrible bond
In the comfortless words, 'waste', 'untimely', 'tragic',
Already gossiped in the obit. conversations.
Good wishes grieve together in the space between us.
It is as if we shall be friends for ever
On the promenades of mourning and insurance,
In whatever sanatoria there are for the spirit,
Sharing the same birthday, the same predestinations.

Fictitious clinics stand by to welcome us,
Prefab'd and windswept on the edge of town
Or bijou in the antiseptic Alps,
In my case the distilled clinic of drink,
The clinic of 'sympathy' and dinners.

We enter a small office. 'What relation?' he asks.
So I tell him. Now come the details he asks for.
A tidy man, with small, hideaway handwriting,
He writes things down. He does not ask,
'Was she good?' Everyone receives this Certificate.
You do not need even to deserve it.
I want to ask why he doesn't look like a saint,
When, across his desk, through his tabulations,
His bureaucracy, his morbid particulars,
The local dead walk into genealogy.
He is no cipher of history, this one,
This recording angel in a green pullover
Administering names and dates and causes.
He has seen all the words that end in -oma.
'You give this to your undertaker.'

When we leave, this time it is by the right door,
A small door, taboo and second-rate.
It is raining. Anonymous brollies go by
In the ubiquitious urban drizzle.
Wedding parties roll up with white ribbons.
Small pools are gathering in the loving bouquets.
They must not see me. I bear a tell-tale scar.
They must not know what I am, or why I am here.
I feel myself digested in statistics of love.
Hundreds of times I must have passed this undertaker's
Sub-gothic premises with leaded windows,
By bus, on foot, by car, paying no attention.
We went past it on our first day in Hull.
Not once did I see someone leave or enter,
And here I am, closing the door behind me,
Turning the corner on a wet day in March.

An Arundel Tomb

Philip Larkin

Side by side, their faces blurred,
The earl and countess lie in stone,
Their proper habits vaguely shown
As jointed armour, stiffened pleat,
And that faint hint of the absurd –
The little dogs under their feet.

Such plainness of the pre-baroque
Hardly involves the eye, until
It meets his left-hand gauntlet, still
Clasped empty in the other; and
One sees, with a sharp tender shock,
His hand withdrawn, holding her hand.

They would not think to lie so long.
Such faithfulness in effigy
Was just a detail friends would see:
A sculptor's sweet commissioned grace
Thrown off in helping to prolong
The Latin names around the base.

They would not guess how early in
Their supine stationary voyage
The air would change to soundless damage,
Turn the old tenantry away;
How soon succeeding eyes begin
To look, not read. Rigidly they

Persisted, linked, through lengths and breadths
Of time. Snow fell, undated. Light
Each summer thronged the glass. A bright
Litter of birdcalls strewed the same
Bone-riddled ground. And up the paths
The endless altered people came,

Washing at their identity.
Now, helpless in the hollow of
An unarmorial age, a trough
Of smoke in slow suspended skeins
Above their scrap of history,
Only an attitude remains:

Time has transfigured them into
Untruth. The stone fidelity
They hardly meant has come to be
Their final blazon, and to prove
Our almost-instinct almost true:
What will survive of us is love.

Romeo and Juliet

William Shakespeare

Characters

Capulet	*Head of the Capulet household in Verona*
Lady Capulet	*His wife and mother of Juliet*
Juliet	*A girl of nearly 14, in love with Romeo of the opposing Montague family*
Nurse	*Servant to the Capulets and Juliet's confidant*

Lady Capulet: But now I'll tell thee joyful tidings, girl.
Juliet: And joy comes well in such a needy time:
   What are they, I beseech your ladyship?
Lady Capulet: Well, well, thou has a careful father, child;
   One who, to put thee from thy heaviness,
   Hath sorted out a sudden day of joy
10   That thou expect'st not, nor I look'd not for.
Juliet: Madam, in happy time! What day is that?
Lady Capulet: Marry, my child, early next Thursday morn
   The gallant, young, and noble gentleman,
   The County Paris, at Saint Peter's church,
15   Shall happily make thee there a joyful bride.
Juliet: Now, by Saint Peter's church, and Peter too,
   He shall not make me there a joyful bride!
   I wonder at this haste; that I must wed
   Ere he that should be husband comes to woo.
20   I pray you, tell my lord and father, madam,
   I will not marry yet; and, when I do, I swear,
   It shall be Romeo, whom you know I hate,
   Rather than Paris. These are news indeed!
Lady Capulet: Here comes your father; tell him so yourself,
   And see how he will take it at your hands.

Enter Capulet and Nurse
Capulet: When the sun sets, the air doth drizzle dew;
But for the sunset of my brother's son
It rains downright.
How now! A conduit, girl? What, still in tears?
130 Evermore showering? In one little body
Thou counterfeit'st a bark, a sea, a wind;
For still thy eyes, which I may call the sea,
Do ebb and flow with tears; the bark thy body is,
Sailing in this salt flood; the winds thy sighs
Who, raging with thy tears, and they with them,
Without a sudden calm, will overset
Thy tempest-tossed body. How now, wife?
Have you deliver'd to her our decree?
Lady Capulet: Ay, sir; but she will none, she gives you thanks.
140 I would the fool were married to her grave!
Capulet: Soft! Take me with you, take me with you, wife.
How? Will she none? Doth she not give us thanks?
Is she not proud? doth she not count her bless'd,
Unworthy as she is, that we have wrought
So worthy a gentleman to be her bride?
Juliet: Not proud you have; but thankful that you have.
Proud can I never be of what I hate;
But thankful even for hate that is meant love.
Capulet: How now, how now? chop-logic! What is this?
150 'Proud', and 'I thank you', and 'I thank you not';
And yet 'not proud'? Mistress minion, you,
Thank me no thankings, nor proud me no prouds,
But fettle your fine joints 'gainst Thursday next,
To go with Paris to Saint Peter's church,
Or I will drag thee on a hurdle thither.
Out, you green-sickness carrion! Out, you baggage!
You tallow-face!
Lady Capulet: Fie, fie! What, are you mad?
Juliet: Good father, I beseech you on my knees,
Hear me with patience but to speak a word.

Capulet: Hang thee, young baggage! Disobedient wretch!
I tell thee what, get thee to church o' Thursday,
Or never after look me in the face.
Speak not, reply not, do not answer me;
My fingers itch. Wife, we scarce thought us bless'd
That God had lent us but this only child;
But now I see this one is one too much,
And that we have a curse in having her.
Out on her, hilding!
Nurse: God in heaven bless her!
You are to blame, my lord, to rate her so.
Capulet: And why, my Lady Wisdom? Hold your tongue,
Good Prudence; smatter with your gossips, go.
Nurse: I speak no treason.
Capulet: O, God ye good e'en.
Nurse: May not one speak?
Capulet: Peace, you mumbling fool!
Utter your gravity o'er a gossip's bowl;
For here we need it not.
Lady Capulet: You are too hot.
Capulet: God's bread! It makes me mad.
Day, night, hour, tide, time, work, play,
Alone, in company – still my care hath been
To have her match'd. And having now provided
A gentleman of noble parentage,
Of fair demesnes, youthful, and nobly lin'd
Stuff'd, as they say, with honourable parts,
Proportion'd as one's thought would wish a man –
And then to have a wretched puling fool,
A whining mammet, in her fortune's tender,
To answer 'I'll not wed, I cannot love,
I am too young, I pray you pardon me'.
But, and you will not wed, I'll pardon you:
Graze where you will, you shall not house with me.
Look to 't, think on 't; I do not use to jest.
Thursday is near. Lay hand on heart; advise.
And you be mine, I'll give you to my friend;
And you be not, hang, beg, starve, die in the streets,

> For, by my soul, I'll ne'er acknowledge thee,
> Nor what is mine shall never do thee good.
> Trust to 't, bethink you. I'll not be forsworn.

Exit

Juliet: Is there no pity sitting in the clouds,
> That sees into the bottom of my grief?
> O sweet my mother, cast me not away!
200 Delay this marriage for a month, a week;
> Or, if you do not, make the bridal bed
> In that dim monument where Tybalt lies.
Lady Capulet: Talk not to me, for I'll not speak a word.
> Do as thou wilt, for I have done with thee.

Exit

Juliet: O God – O Nurse, how shall this be prevented?
> My husband is on earth, my faith in heaven;
> How shall that faith return again to earth,
> Unless that husband sent it me from heaven
> By leaving earth? Comfort me, counsel me.
210 Alack, alack! That heaven should practise strategems
> Upon so soft a subject as myself!
> What sayst thou? Hast thou not a word of joy?
> Some comfort, Nurse?
Nurse: Faith, here it is. Romeo
> Is banished; and all the world to nothing
> That he dares ne'er come back to challenge you;
> Or, if he do, it needs must be by stealth.
> Then, since the case so stands as now it doth,
> I think it best you married with the County.
> O, he's a lovely gentleman!
220 Romeo's a dishclout to him. An eagle, madam,
> Hath not so green, so quick, so fair an eye
> As Paris hath. Beshrew my very heart,
> I think you are happy in this second match,
> For it excels your first: or if it did not,
> Your first is dead – or 'twere as good he were,
> As living here and you no use of him.

Juliet: Speak'st thou from thy heart?
Nurse: And from my soul too;
   Or else beshrew them both.
Juliet: Amen!
Nurse: What!
Juliet: Well, thou hast comforted me marvellous much.
30   Go in; and tell my lady I am gone,
   Having displeas'd my father, to Laurence' cell,
   To make confession and to be absolv'd.
Nurse: Marry, I will; and this is wisely done.

Exit

Juliet: Ancient damnation! O most wicked fiend!
   Is it more sin to wish me thus forsworn,
   Or to dispraise my lord with that same tongue
   Which she hath prais'd him with above compare
   So many thousand times? Go, counsellor!
   Thou and my bosom henceforth shall be twain.
40   I'll to the friar, to know his remedy:
   If all else fail, myself have power to die.

Exit

(Act III, Scene 5, Lines 104–241)

Brothers and Sisters

Alice Walker

We lived on a farm in the South in the fifties, and my brothers, the four of them I knew (the fifth had left home when I was three years old), were allowed to watch animals being mated. This was not unusual; nor was it considered unusual that my older sister and I were frowned upon if we even asked, innocently, what was going on. One of my brothers explained the mating one day, using words my father had given him: 'The bull is getting a little something on his stick,' he said. And he laughed. 'What stick?' I wanted to know. 'Where did he get it? How did he pick it up? Where did he put it?' All my brothers laughed.

I believe my mother's theory about raising a large family of five boys and three girls was that the father should teach the boys and the mother teach the girls the facts, as one says, of life. So my father went around talking about bulls getting something on their sticks and she went around saying girls did not need to know about such things. They were 'womanish' (a very bad way to be in those days) if they asked.

The thing was, watching the matings filled my brothers with an aimless sort of lust, as dangerous as it was unintentional. They knew enough to know that cows, months after mating, produced calves, but they were not bright enough to make the same connection between women and their offspring.

Sometimes, when I think of my childhood, it seems to me a particularly hard one. But in reality, everything awful that happened to me didn't seem to happen to *me* at all, but to my older sister. Through some incredible power to negate my presence around people I did not like, which produced invisibility (as well as an ability to appear mentally vacant when I was nothing of the kind), I was spared the humiliation she was subjected to, though at the same time, I felt every bit of it. It was as if she suffered for my benefit, and I vowed early in my life that none of the things that made existence so miserable for her would happen to me.

The fact that she was not allowed at official matings did not mean she never saw any. While my brothers followed my father to the mating pens on the other side of the road near the barn, she stationed herself near the pigpen, or followed our many dogs until they were in a mating mood, or, failing to witness something there, she watched the chickens. On a farm it is impossible *not* to be conscious of sex, to wonder about it, to dream... but to whom was she to speak of her feelings? Not to my father, who thought all young women perverse. Not to my mother, who pretended all her children grew out of stumps she magically found in the forest. Not to me, who never found anything wrong with this lie.

When my sister menstruated she wore a thick packet of clean rags between her legs. It stuck out in front like a penis. The boys laughed at her as she served them at the table. Not knowing any better, and because our parents did not dream of actually *discussing* what was going on, she would giggle nervously at herself. I hated her for giggling, and it was at those times I would think of her as dim-witted. She never complained, but she began to have strange fainting fits whenever she had her period. Her head felt as if it were splitting, she said, and everything she ate came up again. And her cramps were so severe she could not stand. She was forced to spend several days of each month in bed.

My father expected all of his sons to have sex with women. 'Like bulls,' he said, 'a man *needs* to get a little something on his stick.' And so, on Saturday nights, into town they went, chasing the girls. My sister was rarely allowed into town alone, and if the dress she wore fit too snugly at the waist, or if her cleavage dipped too far below her collarbone, she was made to stay home.

'But why can't I go too,' she would cry, her face screwed up with the effort not to wail.

'They're boys, your brothers, *that's* why they can go.'

Naturally, when she got the chance, she responded eagerly to boys. But when this was discovered she was whipped and locked up in her room.

I would go in to visit her.

'Straight Pine,'[1] she would say, 'you don't know what it *feels* like to want to be loved by a man.'

'And if this is what you get for feeling like it I never will,' I said, with – I hoped – the right combination of sympathy and disgust.

'Men smell so good,' she would whisper ecstatically. 'And when they look into your eyes, you just melt.'

Since they were so hard to catch, naturally she thought almost any of them terrific.

'Oh, that Alfred!' she would moon over some mediocre, square-headed boy, 'he's so *sweet*!' And she would take his ugly picture out of her bosom and kiss it.

My father was always warning her not to come home if she ever found herself pregnant. My mother constantly reminded her that abortion was a sin. Later, although she never became pregnant, her period would not come for months at a time. The painful symptoms, however, never varied or ceased. She fell for the first man who loved her enough to beat her for looking at someone else, and when I was still in high school, she married him.

My fifth brother, the one I never knew, was said to be diffrent from the rest. He had not liked matings. He would not watch them. He thought the cows should be given a choice. My father had disliked him because he was soft. My mother took up for him. 'Jason is just tender-hearted,' she would say in a way that made me know he was her favourite; 'he takes after me.' It was true that my mother cried about almost anything.

Who was this oldest brother? I wondered.

'Well,' said my mother, 'he was someone who always loved you. Of course he was a great big boy when you were born and out working on his own. He worked on a road gang building

---

[1] A pseudonym.

roads. Every morning before he left he would come in the room where you were and pick you up and give you the biggest kisses. He used to look at you and just smile. It's a pity you don't remember him.'

I agreed.

At my father's funeral I finally 'met' my oldest brother. He is tall and black with thick grey hair above a young-looking face. I watched my sister cry over my father until she blacked out from grief. I saw my brothers sobbing, reminding each other of what a great father he had been. My oldest brother and I did not shed a tear between us. When I left my father's grave he came up and introduced himself. 'You don't ever have to walk alone,' he said, and put his arms around me.

One out of five ain't *too* bad, I thought, snuggling up.

But I didn't discover until recently his true uniqueness: He is the only one of my brothers who assumes reponsibility for all his children. The other four all fathered children during those Saturday-night chases of twenty years ago. Children – my nieces and nephews whom I will probably never know – they neither acknowledge as their own, provide for, or even see.

It was not until I became a student of women's liberation ideology that I could understand and forgive my father. I needed an ideology that would define his behaviour in context. The black movement had given me an ideology that helped explain his colourism (he *did* fall in love with my mother partly because she was so light; he never denied it). Feminism helped explain his sexism. I was relieved to know his sexist behaviour was not something uniquely his own, but, rather, an imitation of the behaviour of the society around us.

All partisan movements add to the fullness of our understanding of society as a whole. They never detract; or, in any case, one must not allow them to do so. Experience adds to experience. 'The more things the better,' as O'Connor and Welty both have said, speaking, one of marriage, the other of Catholicism.

I desperately needed my father and brothers to give me male models I could respect, because white men (for example; being particularly handy in this sort of comparison) – whether in films or in person – offered man as dominator, as killer, and always as hypocrite.

My father failed because he copied the hypocrisy. And my brothers – except for one – never understood they must represent half the world to me, and I must represent the other half to them.[2]

[2] Since this essay was written, my brothers have offered their name, acknowledgement, and some support to all their children.

Father to Son

Elizabeth Jennings

I do not understand this child
Though we have lived together now
In the same house for years. I know
Nothing of him, so try to build
Up a relationship from how
He was when small. Yet have I killed

The seed I spent or sown it where
The land is his and none of mine?
We speak like strangers, there's no sign
Of understanding in the air.
This child is built to my design
Yet what he loves I cannot share.

Silence surrounds us. I would have
Him prodigal, returning to
His father's house, the home he knew,
Rather than see him make and move
His world. I would forgive him too,
Shaping from sorrow a new love.

Father and son, we both must live
On the same globe and the same land.
He speaks: I cannot understand
Myself, why anger grows from grief.
We each put out an empty hand,
Longing for something to forgive.

Long Distance

Tony Harrison

I

Your bed's got two wrong sides. Your life's all grouse.
I let your phone-call take its dismal course:

Ah can't stand it no more, this empty house!

Carrots choke us wi'out your mam's white sauce!

Them sweets you brought me, you can have 'em back.
Ah'm diabetic now. Got all the facts.
(The diabetes comes hard on the tracks
of two coronaries and cataracts.)

Ah've allus liked things sweet! But now ah push
food down mi throat! Ah'd sooner do wi'out.
And t'only reason now for beer's to flush
(so t'dietician said) mi kidneys out.

When I come round, they'll be laid out, the sweets,
Lifesavers, my father's New World treats,
still in the big brown bag, and only bought
rushing through JFK as a last thought.

II

Though my mother was already two years dead
Dad kept her slippers warming by the gas,
put hot water bottles her side of the bed
and still went to renew her transport pass.

Long Distance

You couldn't just drop in. You had to phone.
He'd put you off an hour to give him time
to clear away her things and look alone
as though his still raw love were such a crime.

He couldn't risk my blight of disbelief
though sure that very soon he'd hear her key
scrape in the rusted lock and end his grief.
He *knew* she'd just popped out to get the tea.

I believe life ends with death, and that is all.
You haven't both gone shopping; just the same,
in my new black leather phone book there's your name
and the disconnected number I still call.

Flight

Doris Lessing

Above the old man's head was the dovecote, a tall wire-netted shelf on stilts, full of strutting, preening birds. The sunlight broke on their grey breasts into small rainbows. His ears were lulled by their crooning, his hands stretched up towards the favourite, a homing pigeon, a young plump-bodied bird which stood still when it saw him and cocked a shrewd bright eye.

'Pretty, pretty, pretty,' he said, as he grasped the bird and drew it down, feeling the cold coral claws tighten around his finger. Content, he rested the bird lightly on his chest, and leaned against a tree, gazing out beyond the dovecote into the landscape of a late afternoon. In folds and hollows of sunlight and shade, the dark red soil, which was broken into great dusty clods, stretched wide to a tall horizon. Trees marked the course of the valley; a stream of rich green grass the road.

His eyes travelled homewards along this road until he saw his granddaughter swinging on the gate underneath a frangipani tree. Her hair fell down her back in a wave of sunlight, and her long bare legs repeated the angles of the frangipani stems, bare, shining-brown stems among patterns of pale blossoms.

She was gazing past the pink flowers, past the railway cottage where they lived, along the road to the village.

His mood shifted. He deliberately held out his wrist for the bird to take flight, and caught it again at the moment it spread its wings. He felt the plump shape strive and strain under his fingers; and, in a sudden access of troubled spite, shut the bird into a small box and fastened the bolt. 'Now you stay there,' he muttered; and turned his back on the shelf of birds. He moved warily along the hedge, stalking his grand-daughter, who was now looped over the gate, her head loose on her arms, singing. The light happy sound mingled with the crooning of the birds, and his anger mounted.

'Hey!' he shouted; saw her jump, look back, and abandon the gate. Her eyes veiled themselves, and she said in a pert neutral voice: 'Hullo, Grandad.' Politely she moved towards him, after a lingering backward glance at the road.

'Waiting for Steven, hey?' he said, his fingers curling like claws into his palm.

'Any objection?' she asked lightly, refusing to look at him.

He confronted her, his eyes narrowed, shoulders hunched, tight in a hard knot of pain which included the preening birds, the sunlight, the flowers. He said: 'Think you're old enough to go courting, hey?'

The girl tossed her head at the old-fashioned phrase and sulked, 'Oh, Grandad!'

'Think you want to leave home, hey? Think you can go running around the fields at night?'

Her smile made him see her, as he had every evening of this warm end-of-summer month, swinging hand in hand along the road to the village with that red-handed, red-throated, violent-bodied youth, the son of the postmaster. Misery went to his head and he shouted angrily: 'I'll tell your mother!'

'Tell away!' she said, laughing, and went back to the gate.

He heard her singing, for him to hear:

'I've got you under my skin,
I've got you deep in the heart of...'

'Rubbish,' he shouted. 'Rubbish. Impudent little bit of rubbish!'

Growling under his breath he turned towards the dovecote, which was his refuge from the house he shared with his daughter and her husband and their children. But now the house would be empty. Gone all the young girls with their laughter and their squabbling and their teasing. He would be left, uncherished and alone, with that square-fronted, calm-eyed woman, his daughter.

He stooped, muttering, before the dovecote, resenting the absorbed cooing birds.

From the gate the girl shouted: 'Go and tell! Go on, what are you waiting for?'

Obstinately he made his way to the house, with quick, pathetic persistent glances of appeal back at her. But she never looked around. Her defiant but anxious young body stung him into love and repentance. He stopped. 'But I never meant...' he muttered, waiting for her to turn and run to him. 'I didn't mean...'

She did not turn. She had forgotten him. Along the road came the young man Steven, with something in his hand. A present for her? The old man stiffened as he watched the gate swing back, and the couple embrace. In the brittle shadows of the frangipani tree his granddaughter, his darling, lay in the arms of the postmaster's son, and her hair flowed back over his shoulder.

'I see you!' shouted the old man spitefully. They did not move. He stumped into the little whitewashed house, hearing the wooden veranda creak angrily under his feet. His daughter was sewing in the front room, threading a needle held to the light.

He stopped again, looking back into the garden. The couple were now sauntering among the bushes, laughing. As he watched he saw the girl escape from the youth with a sudden mischievous movement, and run off through the flowers with him in pursuit. He heard shouts, laughter, a scream, silence.

'But it's not like that at all,' he muttered miserably. 'It's not like that. Why can't you see? Running and giggling, and kissing and kissing. You'll come to something quite different.'

He looked at his daughter with sardonic hatred, hating himself. They were caught and finished, both of them, but the girl was still running free.

'Can't you *see*?' he demanded of his invisible granddaughter, who was at that moment lying in the thick green grass with the postmaster's son.

His daughter looked at him and her eyebrows went up in tired forbearance.

'Put your birds to bed?' she asked, humouring him.

'Lucy,' he said urgently. 'Lucy...'

'Well, what is it now?'

'She's in the garden with Steven.'

'Now you just sit down and have your tea.'

He stumped his feet alternatively, thump, thump, on the hollow wooden floor and shouted: 'She'll marry him. I'm telling you, she'll be marrying him next!'

His daughter rose swiftly, brought him a cup, set him a plate.

'I don't want any tea. I don't want it, I tell you.'

'Now, now,' she crooned. 'What's wrong with it? Why not?'

'She's eighteen. Eighteen!'

'I was married at seventeen and I never regretted it.'

'Liar,' he said. 'Liar. Then you should regret it. Why do you make your girls marry? It's you who do it. What do you do it for? Why?'

'The other three have done fine. They've three fine husbands. Why not Alice?'

'She's the last,' he mourned. 'Can't we keep her a bit longer?'

'Come, now, dad. She'll be down the road, that's all. She'll be here every day to see you.'

'But it's not the same.' He thought of the other three girls, transformed inside a few months from charming petulant spoiled children into serious young matrons.

'You never did like it when we married,' she said. 'Why not? Every time, it's the same. When I got married you made me feel like it was something wrong. And my girls the same. You get them all crying and miserable the way you go on. Leave Alice alone. She's happy.' She sighed, letting her eyes linger on the sunlit garden. 'She'll marry next month. There's no reason to wait.'

'You've said they can marry?' he said incredulously.

'Yes, dad, why not?' she said coldly, and took up her sewing.

His eyes stung, and he went out on to the veranda. Wet spread down over his chin and he took out a handkerchief and mopped his whole face. The garden was empty.

From around the corner came the young couple; but their faces were no longer set against him. On the wrist of the postmaster's son balanced a young pigeon, the light gleaming on its breast.

'For me?' said the old man, letting the drops shake off his chin. 'For me?'

'Do you like it?' The girl grabbed his hand and swung on it. 'It's for you, Grandad. Steven brought it for you.' They hung about him, affectionate, concerned, trying to charm away his wet eyes and his misery. They took his arms and directed him to the shelf of birds, one on each side, enclosing him, petting him, saying worldlessly that nothing would be changed, nothing could change, and that they would be with him always. The bird was proof of it, they said, from their lying happy eyes, as they thrust it on him. 'There, Grandad, it's yours. It's for you.'

They watched him as he held it on his wrist, stroking its soft, sun-warmed back, watching the wings lift and balance.

'You must shut it up for a bit,' said the girl intimately. 'Until it knows this is its home.'

'Teach your grandmother to suck eggs,' growled the old man.

Released by his half-deliberate anger, they fell back, laughing at him. 'We're glad you like it.' They moved off, now serious and full of purpose, to the gate, where they hung, backs to him, talking quietly. More than anything could, their grown-up seriousness shut him out, making him alone; also, it quietened him, took the sting out of their tumbling like puppies on the grass. They had forgotten him again. Well, so they should, the old man reassured himself, feeling his throat clotted with tears, his lips trembling. He held the new bird to his face, for the caress of its silken feathers. Then he shut it in a box and took out his favourite.

'*Now* you can go,' he said aloud. He held it poised, ready for flight, while he looked down the garden towards the boy and the girl. Then, clenched in the pain of loss, he lifted the bird on his wrist, and watched it soar. A whirr and a spatter of wings, and a cloud of birds rose into the evening from the dovecote.

At the gate Alice and Steven forgot their talk and watched the birds.

On the veranda, that woman, his daughter, stood gazing, her eyes shaded with a hand that still held her sewing.

It seemed to the old man that the whole afternoon had stilled to watch his gesture of self-command, that even the leaves of the trees had stopped shaking.

Dry-eyed and calm, he let his hands fall to his sides and stood erect, staring up into the sky.

The cloud of shining silver birds flew up and up, with a shrill cleaving of wings, over the dark ploughed land and the darker belts of trees and the bright folds of grass, until they floated high in the sunlight, like a cloud of motes of dust.

They wheeled in a wide circle, tilting their wings so there was flash after flash of light, and one after another they dropped from the sunshine of the upper sky to shadow, one after another, returning to the shadowed earth over trees and grass and field, returning to the valley and the shelter of night.

The garden was all a fluster and a flurry of returning birds. Then silence, and the sky was empty.

The old man turned, slowly, taking his time; he lifted his eyes to smile proudly down the garden at his granddaughter. She was staring at him. She did not smile. She was wide-eyed, and pale in the cold shadow, and he saw the tears run shivering off her face.

Death of an Old Dog

Antonia Fraser

Paulina Gavin came back from the vet with a sweet expression on her heart-shaped face. The little crease which sometimes – just slightly – marred the smooth white skin between her brows was absent. Her eyes, grey yet soft, swept round the sitting room. Then they came to rest, lovingly, on Richard.

'Darling, I'm late! But supper won't be late. I've got it all planned.'

Widowhood had made of Richard Gavin a good, as well as a quick cook. But Paulina had not seen fit to call on his talents before her visit to the vet: he found no note of instructions awaiting him. Now Paulina kissed him with delicious pressure on his cheek, just where his thick grizzled sideburn ended. It was her special place.

From this, Richard knew that Ibo was condemned to die.

Viewing the situation with detachment, as befitted a leading barrister, Richard was not the slightest bit surprised that the verdict should have gone against Ibo. The forces ranged against each other were simply not equal. On the one side, the vet, in his twenties, and Paulina, not much older. On the other side, Ibo. And Ibo was not merely old. He was a very old dog indeed.

He dated from the early days of Richard's first marriage, and that balmy period not only seemed a great while since, a long, long time ago (in the words of Richard's favourite quotation from Ford) but actually was. Even the origin of the nickname Ibo was lost in some private joke of his marriage to Grace: as far as he could remember the dog had begun as Hippolytus. Was it an allusion to his sympathies in the Nigerian Civil War? Based on the fact that Ibo, like the Biafrans, was always starving... That too seemed a long, long time ago.

You could therefore say sentimentally that Ibo and Richard had grown old together. Except that it would not actually be true.

For Richard had gingerly put out one toe towards middle age, only to be dragged backwards by Paulina's rounded arms, her curiously strong little hands. And having been rescued, Richard was obviously reposited in the prime of life, as though on a throne.

His past athletic prowess (including a really first-class tennis game which only pressure at the Bar had prevented him taking further) was easy to recall, looking at his tall, trim figure. If anything, he had lost weight recently. And it was not only the endearing Paulina but Richard's friends who generally described him as 'handsomer than ever'. It was as though the twenty-five-year age gap between Richard and his second wife had acted upon him as a rejuvenating injection.

The same miracle had not been performed for the master's dog. Casting his mind back, Richard could dimly recall embarrassing walks in the park with Ibo, portrait of a young dog at the evident height of his amorous powers. Now the most desirable spaniel bitch would flaunt herself in vain before him. Like Boxer in *Animal Farm*, where energy was concerned, Ibo was merely a shadow of his former self. And he did not even have Boxer's tragic dignity. Ibo by now was just a very shaggy and, to face the facts fully, a very smelly old dog.

Richard stirred in his chair. The topic must be raised. Besides, he had another important subject to discuss with Paulina, sooner or later.

'How did you get on at the vet, darling?' he called. She had after all not yet mentioned her visit.

But Paulina, having skipped into the kitchen, apparently did not hear. Pre-arranged odours were wafting from it. Richard guessed that she would soon emerge having removed her apron. He guessed that she would be bearing with her a bottle of red wine, already opened, and two glasses on a tray. There was, he suspected, a strong possibility that supper would be eaten by candle-light.

Both guesses were correct. The suspicion was confirmed when Paulina artlessly discovered some candles left over from Christmas and decided on impulse to use them up.

'Why not? Just for us,' she enquired to no one in particular, as she sat down at the now positively festive little table with its browny-red casserole, its red Beaujolais and scarlet candles. Then Paulina's manner quite changed.

'Poor Ibo,' sighed Paulina, 'I'm afraid the vet didn't hold out much hope.'

'Hope?' repeated Richard in a surprised voice. It was not surely a question of *hope* – what hope could there possibly be for a very old, very smelly dog? – but of life. It was the continuation of Ibo's life they were discussing, for that was all he had to expect, not the possibility of his magical rejuvenation.

'Well, *hope*,' repeated Paulina in her turn, sounding for the first time ruffled, as though the conversation had taken an unexpected and therefore unwelcome turn. 'Hope is so important, isn't it? Without hope, I don't see much point in any of us going on —'

But Richard's attention was distracted. There was an absence. He would have noticed it immediately had it not been for Paulina's charade with the dinner.

Where was Ibo? Obese, waddling, grey-muzzled, frequently flea-ridden, half-blind, where was Ibo? Normally his first action on entering the sitting room would have been to kiss, no, slobber over, Richard's hand. Then Ibo, an optimist, might have wagged his stumpy tail as though, despite the lateness of the hour and his incapacity, a walk was in the offing. Finally, convinced of his own absurdity, he would have made for the fire, pausing for a last lick of Richard's hand. None of this had happened. Where was Ibo?

Paulina began to speak quickly, muttering things about further tests, the young vet's kindness, the need to take a dispassionate decision, and so forth, which all seemed to add up to the fact that the vet had kept the dog in over-night. Once again Richard cut in.

'You do realize Toddie comes home from school tomorrow?'

This time an expression of sheer panic crossed Paulina's face. It was only too obvious she had quite forgotten.

'How can he be?' she began. 'He's only just gone there —' She stopped. She had remembered. Toddie, the strange silent ten-year-old son of Richard's first marriage, was returning the next day from school to have his new plate tightened. The dentist had emphasized that the appointments had to be regular, and had thus overruled protests from Richard who wanted Toddie to wait for half-term. At first Toddie had taken the news of his quick turn round with his usual imperturbability. But after a moment he had suddenly knelt down and flung his arms round, Ibo, a mat of fur before the fire.

'Then I'll be seeing you very soon again, won't I, you good old boy? The best dog in the world.' It was a long speech for Toddie.

Toddie's embraces were reserved exclusively for Ibo. His father had tried a few grave kisses after Grace's death. Toddie held himself rigid as though under attack. Later they had settled for ritual handshakes. When Richard married Paulina he had advised her against any form of affectionate assault on Toddie, warned by his own experiences. For Paulina, the frequent light kiss was as natural a mode of communication as Richard's solemn handshake. Baulked of this, she had ended up deprived of any physical contact at all with Toddie. At first it worried her: a motherless boy... Later, as her step-son remained taciturn, not so much a motherless boy as an inscrutable person, she was secretly glad she was not committed to hugging and kissing this enigma with his unsmiling lips, and disconcertingly expressionless eyes.

Only two things provoked any kind of visible reaction from Toddie. One was crime, murder to be precise. No doubt it was a natural concomitant to his father's career. But Paulina sometimes found the spectacle of Toddie poring over the newspaper in search of some gruesome trial rather distasteful. It was true that he concentrated on the law reports, showing, for example, considerable knowledge of appeal procedure, rather than on the horror stories in the popular press. Perhaps he would grow up to be a barrister like Richard... In which case, where murder was concerned, he was making a flying start.

Toddie's other visible interest was of course Ibo.

Jolted by the prospect of the boy's return, Paulina now launched into a flood of explanation concerning the true nature of Ibo's condition. Ibo had a large growth, said the vet. Hadn't they noticed it? Richard clenched his hands. How long since he had brought himself to examine Ibo? Ibo simply existed. Or had simply existed up to the present time. Paulina went on to outline the case, extremely lucidly, for 'putting Ibo out of his misery' as she phrased it. Or rather, to be honest, sparing him the misery that was to come. Nobody pretended that Ibo was in violent misery now, a little discomfort perhaps. But he would shortly *be* in misery, that was the point. Richard listened carefully and without surprise. Had he not known since the moment that his wife pressed her lips to his cheek that Ibo was condemned to die?

What Richard Gavin had not realized, and did not realize until he conceded, judicially, regretfully, the case for Ibo's demise, was that the old dog was not actually condemned to die. He was already dead. Had been dead throughout all the fairly long discussion. Had been put to sleep by the vet that very afternoon on the authority, the sole authority, of Paulina Gavin. Who had then returned audaciously, almost flirtatiously, to argue her senior and distinguished husband round to her own point of view...

The look on the face of Richard Gavin, QC, was for one instant quite terrible. But Paulina held up her own quite bravely. With patience – she was not nearly so frightened of Richard now as she had been when they first married – she pointed out to her husband the wisdom and even kindness of her strategy. Someone had to make the decision, and so she, Paulina, had made it. In so doing, she had removed from Richard the hideous, the painful necessity of condemning to death an old friend, a dear old friend. It was much easier for her – Richard had after all known Ibo for so much longer. Yet since Richard was such a rational man and loved to think every decision through, she had felt she owed it to him to argue it all out.

'Confident of course that you would make your case?'

Richard's voice sounded guarded, as his voice did sometimes in court, during a cross-examination. His expression was quite blank: for a moment he reminded Paulina uncomfortably of Toddie. But she stuck firmly to her last.

'I know I was right, darling,' she said, 'I acted for the best. You'll see. Someone had to decide.'

There remained the problem of Toddie's precipitate return, the one factor which, to be honest, Paulina had left out of her calculations. She had expected to be able to break the sad news at half-term, a decent interval away. But the next morning, Paulina, pretty as a picture in a gingham house-dress at breakfast, made it clear that she could cope with that too. With brightness she handed Richard his mail:

'*Personal and Confidential*! Is it the bank?'

With brightness she let it be understood that it was she, Paulina, who would sacrifice her day at the office – the designers' studio she ran with such *élan* – to ferry Toddie to and from school. Although she had already sacrificed an afternoon going to the vet. The only thing Richard was expected to do, Paulina rattled on, was to return from *his* office, in other words his chambers, in the afternoon and tell his son the news about the dog.

Richard continued to wear his habitual morning expression, a frown apparently produced by his mail:

'No, it's not the bank,' he said.

'Income Tax, then?' Paulina was determined to make conversation.

'No.'

'Some case, I suppose.'

'You could put it like that.'

'Why here? Why not to your chambers?' Paulina carried on chattily.

'Paulina,' said Richard, pushing back his chair and rising. 'You must understand that I don't exactly look forward to telling Toddie that Ibo is dead.'

'Oh God, darling,' cried Paulina, jumping up in her turn, her eyes starting with bright tears, 'I know, I know, I *know*.' She hugged all that was reachable of his imposing figure. 'But it was for *him*.'

'For Ibo?'

'Yes, for him. That poor dear old fellow. Poor, poor old Ibo. I know, I understand. It's the saddest thing in the world, the death of an old dog. But it is – somehow, isn't it, darling? – inevitable.'

The hugging came to an end, and then Paulina dried her tears. Richard went off to his study, the large book-lined room which Paulina had created for him above the garage. He indicated that he would telephone his clerk with a view to taking the whole day off from his chambers.

One of the features of the study was a large picture window which faced out at the back over the fields to the wood. To protect Richard's privacy, the study had no windows overlooking the house. There was merely a brick façade. This morning, Paulina suddenly felt that both the study and Richard were turning their back on her. But that was fanciful. She was overwrought on account of poor Toddie. And of course poor Ibo.

Paulina reminded herself that she too was not without her feelings, her own fondness for the wretched animal. It had been a brave and resolute thing she had done to spare Richard, something of which she would not have been capable a few years back. How much the studio had done for her self-confidence! Nerves calmed by the contemplation of her new wise maturity, Paulina got the car out of the garage and went off to fetch Toddie.

Of course Toddie knew something was wrong the moment he entered the empty house. He slipped out of the car and ran across the courtyard the moment they returned; although by reparking the car in the garage immediately, Paulina had hoped to propel him straight into his father's care. As it was, she refused to answer Toddie's agitated question as to why Ibo did not come to greet him. She simply took him by the shoulder and led him back as fast as possible to the garage. Then it was up the stairs and into the study. Paulina did not intend to linger. She had no wish to witness the moment of Toddie's breakdown.

She had once asked Richard how Toddie took the news of his mother's death, so sudden, so appalling, in a road accident on the way to pick him up at kindergarten.

'He howled,' Richard replied.

'You mean, cried and cried.'

'No, howled. Howled once. One terrible howl, then nothing. Just as if someone had put their hand across his mouth to stop him. It was a howl like a dog.'

Paulina shuddered. It was a most distasteful comparison to recall at the present moment. She was by now at the head of the narrow staircase and thrusting Toddie into the big book-lined room with it vast window. But before she could leave, Richard was saying in that firm voice she recognized from the courts:

'Toddie, you know about the law, don't you?'

The boy nodded and stared.

'Well, I want you to know that there has been a trial here. The trial of Ibo.' Toddie continued to stare, his large round eyes almost fish-like. Paulina turned and fled away down the stairs. No doubt Richard knew his own business – and his own son – best. But to her it sounded a most ghoulish way of breaking the news.

A greal deal of time passed; time enough for Paulina to speak several times to her office (pleasingly incapable of managing without her); time enough for Paulina to reflect how very unused she had become to a housewife's enforced idleness, waiting on the movements of the males of the family. She tried to fill the gap by making an interesting tea for Toddie, in case that might solace him. But it was in fact long past tea-time when Paulina finally received some signal from the study across the way. She was just thinking that if Richard did not emerge soon, she would be late returning Toddie to Graybanks (and that would hardly help him recover) when the bleep-bleep of the intercom roused her.

'He's coming down,' said Richard's voice, slightly distorted by the wire which crackled. 'Naturally he doesn't want to talk about it, so would you take him straight back to school? As soon as possible. No, no tea, thank you. He'll be waiting for you in the car.' And that was all. The intercom clicked off.

Upset, in spite of herself, by Richard's brusqueness, Paulina hastily put away the interesting tea as best she could. Still fighting down her feelings, she hurried to put on her jacket and re-cross the courtyard. But she could not quite extinguish all resentment. It was lucky, she thought crossly, that as Richard grew older he would have a tactful young wife at his elbow; that should preserve him from those slight rigidities, or perhaps acidities was a better word, to which all successful men were prone after a certain age. For the second time that day she recalled with satisfaction the moral courage she had shown in having Ibo put down on her own initiative without distressing her husband; there was no doubt that Richard was relying on her already.

This consciousness of virtue enabled her – but only just – to stifle her irritation at the fact that Richard had not even bothered to open the big garage doors for her. Really, men were the most ungrateful creatures; it was she, not Richard, who was facing a cross-country journey in the dark; he might at least have shown his normal chivalry to ease her on her way – taking back his son, not hers, to school. Reliance was one thing, dependence and over-dependence quite another. Still in an oddly perturbed mood for one normally so calm and competent, Paulina slipped through the door which led to the garage.

She went towards the car. She was surprised that the engine was already running. And Toddie was not in the passenger seat. In fact the car appeared to be empty. She tried the door. It was locked. Behind her was the noise of the little side-door shutting.

About the same time Richard Gavin was thinking that he would miss Paulina, he really would: her cooking, her pretty ways, her office gossip. Habit had even reconciled him to the last. In many ways she had been a delightful even a delicious wife for a successful man. The trouble was that she clearly would not make any sort of wife for an older man dying slowly and probably painfully of an incurable disease. This morning the doctors had finally given him no hope. He had been waiting for the last hope to vanish, putting off the moment, before sharing the fearful burden with her.

Really, her ruthless and overbearing behaviour over poor Ibo had been a blessing in disguise. For it had opened his eyes just in time. No, Paulina would certainly not be the kind of wife to solace her husband's protracted deathbed. She might even prove to be the dreadful sort of person who believed in euthanasia 'to put him out of his misery'. He corrected himself. Paulina might even *have* proved to be such a person.

Back in the garage, the smell of exhaust fumes soon began to fill the air. Still no one came to open the garage doors. Even the side-door was now apparently locked from the outside. Paulina's last conscious thought, fighting in vain to get the garage doors open, was that she would really have to arrange automatic openers one of these days – now that Richard was no longer as young as he was, no longer eager to help her.

A couple of fields away, in a copse, Toddie was showing his father the exact spot where he would like to have Ibo buried. Richard had been quite desperate as he would tell the police later, to cheer the poor little chap up. It was a natural, if sentimental expedition for a father to make with his son. A son so bereft by the death of an old dog. A son so early traumatized by the death of his mother (a step-mother was not at all the same thing, alas).

And when the police came, as they surely would, to the regrettable conclusion that the second Mrs Gavin's death had not in fact been an accident, well, it really all added up, didn't it? Exactly the same factors came into play and would be ably, amply, interminably examined by the long list of child psychiatrists to whom Toddie would be inevitably subjected.

But Toddie, Richard reflected with a certain professional detachment, would be more than a match for them. What interested him most about his son was his burning desire to get on with the business of confessing his crime. He seemed to be positively looking forward to his involvement with the police and so forth. He was certainly very satisfied with the way he had compassed his step-mother's death.

Richard was also quite surprised at the extent of Toddie's knowledge of the law concerning murderers. You could almost say that Toddie had specialized in the subject. Whereas he himself had never had much to do with that line of country.

Richard realized suddenly that it was the first time he had ever really felt interested by his son.

Under the circumstances, Toddie very much doubted that he would have to spend many years in prison. He intended to end up as a model prisoner. But there might have to be a bad patch from which he could be redeemed: otherwise he might not present an interesting enough case, and the interesting cases always got out first. No, Toddie really had it all worked out.

'Besides, Dad,' ended Toddie, no longer in the slightest bit taciturn, 'I'm proud of what I did. You told me how to do it. But I'd have done it somehow anyway. She deserved to die. She condemned Ibo to death without telling us. Behind our backs. No proper trial. And killed him. Ibo, the best dog in the world.'

The Lady Who Loved Insects

Anon (translated by Arthur Waley)

Next door to the lady who loved butterflies was the house of a certain provincial inspector. He had an only daugher, to whose upbringing he and his wife devoted endless care. She was a strange girl, and used to say: 'Why do people make so much fuss about butterflies and never give a thought to the creatures out of which butterflies grow? It is the natural form of things that is always the most important.' She collected all kinds of reptiles and insects such as most people are frightened to touch, and watched them day by day to see what they would turn into, keeping them in various sorts of little boxes and cages. Among all these creatures her favourite was the common caterpillar. Hour after hour, her hair pushed back from her eyes, she would sit gazing at the furry black form that nestled in the palm of her hand. She found that other girls were frightened of these pets, and her only companions were a number of rather rough little boys, who were not in the least afraid. She got them to carry about the insect-boxes, find out the names of the insects or, if this could not be done, help her to give them new names. She hated anything that was not natural. Consequently she would not pluck a single hair from her eyebrows nor would she blacken her teeth, saying it was a dirty and disagreeable custom. So morning, noon, and night she tended her insects, bending over them with a strange, white gleaming smile.[1] People on the whole were frightened of her and kept away; the few who ventured to approach her came back with the strangest reports. If anyone showed the slightest distaste for her pets, she would ask him indignantly how he could give way to so silly and vulgar a prejudice, and as she said this she would stare at the visitor

---

[1] Because of her unblackened teeth.

under her black, bushy eyebrows in a way that made him feel extremely uncomfortable.

Her parents thought all this very peculiar and would much rather she had been more like other children; but they saw it was no use arguing with her. She for her part took immense trouble in explaining her ideas, but this only resulted in making them feel that she was much cleverer than they. 'No doubt,' they would say, 'all you tell us is quite true, and so far as we are concerned you may do as you please. But people as a rule only make pets of charming and pretty things. If it gets about that you keep hairy caterpillars you will be thought a disgusting girl and no one will want to know you.' 'I do not mind what they think,' she answered. 'I want to inquire into everything that exists and find out how it began. Nothing else interests me. And it is very silly of them to dislike caterpillars, all of which will soon turn into lovely butterflies.' Then she again explained to them carefully how the cocoon, which is like the thick winter clothes that human beings wear, wraps up the caterpillar till its wings have grown and it is ready to be a butterfly. Then it suddenly waves its white sleeves and flits away...

This was no doubt quite accurate, and they could think of nothing to say in reply; but all the same her views on such matters made them feel very uncomfortable. She would never sit in the same room with her elders, quoting in self-defence the proverb, 'Ghosts and girls are best unseen'; and the above attempt to bring her parents to reason was made through a chink in the half-raised blinds of the living room. Hearing of such conversations as this, the young people of the district were amazed at the profundity of her researches. 'But what things for a girl to play with!' they said. 'She must be an oddity indeed. Let us go and call upon the girl who loves butterflies.'

Hearing some of the unflattering comparisons that were being made between herself and the butterfly lady, she rejoined: 'I do not see anything very admirable in making a fuss over butterflies. Even those young men must know by now that the prettiest butterflies are but the sheddings of creatures like my hairy caterpillars, who discard them as a snake drops its skin. And

The Lady Who Loved Insects

caterpillars are much friendlier playthings. For if you catch hold of a butterfly it frees itself as soon as it can, leaving its golden powder on your hand, and this powder is very dangerous, often causing fevers and agues. Fancy trying to make pets of butterflies! It is horrible to think of.'

To the little boys who formed her retinue she would give pretty things such as she knew they wanted, and in return they would give her all kinds of terrifying insects. She said the caterpillars would be unhappy if there were no creatures with them to admire their glossy coats, and she therefore collected a number of snails, and also of grass-crickets whose ferocious and incessant cries seemed to suggest that they were at war with one another, thus recalling to her mind the line, 'For the ground between a snail's horns what use to fight?'[2] She said she was tired of ordinary boys' names and called her servitors by insect-names, such as Kerao (mole-cricket boy), Inagomaro (locust-man), Amabiko (centipede), and the like. All this was thought very queer and stupid.

Among those who had heard gossip about the girl and her odd pets was a certain young man of good family who vowed that, fond of strange creatures though she might be, he would undertake to give her a fright. So saying he made a marvellously lifelike snake with joints that moved and putting it into a scaly bag sent it to her with the poem: 'Creeping and crawling I shall sneak my way to your side, for my persistence[3] is tireless as my body is long.' The servant who brought the bag had no idea what it contained. 'I wonder what can be in it,' he said, as he untied the string. 'Certainly something remarkably heavy!' The bag was opened, and to the horror of everyone present a snake protruded its head. But the lady was not at all put out, and having repeated several times the prayer *Namu Amida Butsu* she said, 'Do not be frightened! Remember that any one of you may have been a snake in his former existence. Look at the kindly expression of his face and how he is making himself tremble all down his back.

---

[2] From one of five drinking songs written by the Chinese poet Po Chü-i about 829.

[3] 'Persistence' is 'length of heart' (*kokoro-nagasa*) in Japanese.

Could anything be clearer than that he is signalling to you not to be afraid? I am amazed that anyone should not understand him.' So she muttered to herself, and drew the bag toward her. But all the same it seemed as though even she were a little afraid, for now she hovered near the creature and now fluttered away again, like a moth at the candle, crooning to it all the while in a low insect voice.

Seeing several of the servants rush out of her room tumbling over one another and screaming with laughter the lady's father asked them what had happened, and at the mention of a snake exclaimed in great consternation, 'A nice trick to play upon a young woman! I cannot understand anyone doing such a dastardly thing. A fine pack of rascals you are, to run off like this and leave her with a dangerous viper in the room.' So saying, he seized his sword and brandishing it over his head rushed to his daughter's side. But the moment he saw the snake a doubt crossed his mind and examining it attentively he discovered it was only an extremely well-made toy. Picking it up he said, 'I remember now that I have heard people say how clever the fellow is at making things of this sort. You must be sure to write at once and thank him for his kindness.' When it was known that the snake was only a toy the people who had run away from it declared the joke to be a very silly one. But the lady agreed that it would be rude not to reply and taking a stout, sensible-looking sheet of paper she wrote the following poem, not in *hiragana*, which she never used, but in *katakana*:[4] 'If indeed we are fated to meet, not here will it be, but in Paradise, thou crafty image of a snake.' And at the side was written: 'In the Garden of Blessings you must plant your seed.'[5]

It happened that a certain Captain of Horse saw this letter and being much struck with it he determined to obtain an interview with the writer. Choosing a time when he knew her father to be busy elsewhere, he posted himself at a wattled gate on the

[4] A square, in elegant, but eminently 'sensible' form of syllabary, now used for telegrams, etc.
[5] The snake must by good behaviour get itself reborn in some more dignified incarnation.

woman's side of the house and peeped in. Several little boys were poking about among some very dull-looking bushes and shrubs. Presently one of them called out, 'Just look at these bushes! They're simply covered with creatures. It's the best place we have ever found.' And going to the window he pulled the blind. 'Do look at them,' he said again. 'You can see them from the window. Aren't they the loveliest caterpillars you ever saw?' 'Yes, they're not at all bad,' said a voice from within. 'you may bring them in here if you like.' 'I've nothing to put them in,' said the boy. 'You must look at them where they are.' Presently the blind was pulled right aside and a girl appeared at the window, craning out toward the nearest boughs of the shrubbery. She had pulled her mantle over her head, but her hair hung loose beneath it, and very lovely hair it was too, but rather untidy-looking, and the Captain thought it must be a long time since she had combed it. Her thick, very dark eyebrows gave her face a rather forbidding air. Her other features were by no means bad. But when she smiled her white teeth gleamed and flashed in a manner that rather digusted him, for there was something wild and barbaric about it.

'What a sad case!' thought the Captain. 'If only she took an ordinary amount of trouble with herself she really would not be bad-looking.' Even as she was he did not find her altogether unattractive; for there was about her a strange kind of vehemence, a liveliness of expression, a brilliance of complexion and colouring that could not fail to make some impression on him. With her clothes in themselves there was nothing wrong. She wore a robe of soft, glossy silk, with a spinner's jacket, and white trousers. In order to get a good view of the caterpillars she leaned right out of the window, crying, 'Aren't they clever! They've come here in order to be out of the sun. Boy, you might just bring me that one there. I should like to have a better look at him. Be sure not to let him fall.' Upon which the boy at once bumped into something and the caterpillar fell with a thud upon the ground. She then handed him a white fan with some Chinese characters written upon it in black ink, saying, 'Pick him up quickly and carry him in on this.'

It was only now that she caught sight of the Captain, who was still loitering at the wicker gate. To see anyone there was a considerable surprise, for the young men of the neighbourhood had long ago decided that she was what they called 'a disastrous character', and it was seldom indeed that anyone came that way. The little boy, too, had become aware of the visitor's presence and cried out in astonishment, 'Look, there's a gentleman standing at the wicker gate. I can't make out what he is doing. He seems to be staring at us.' One of the maids now came along and began to scold her. 'fie upon you,' she said, 'I shall go straight to your father and tell him you're busy with your nasty insects again, and leaning right out of the window where anyone can see you.' But the girl continued to fiddle about with the hairy caterpillars on the bushes near the window. The maid, who had a horror of such creatures, was far too frightened to come any closer, but called again, 'Madam, go in this instant. You can be seen!' 'Well, what if I can be seen? I am not doing anything to be ashamed of.' 'I'm not joking, I assure you,' said the maid indignantly. 'There's a fine gentleman standing right there at the gate. Go away from the window at once!' 'Kerao,' said the girl at last, 'just go to the gate and see if there is still someone there.' He ran a little distance toward the gate and presently called out, 'It's quite true, there is somebody'. Upon which she gathered several caterpillars in her sleeve and stepped back into the interior of the house.

For a moment he saw her at full length. She was rather tall. Her hair floated out behind her as she moved. It was very thick, but the ends were somewhat wispy, no doubt through lack of trimming. But with a little more looking after it would have made (he thought) a fine crop of hair. Certainly she was no great beauty, but if she dressed and behaved like other people she would, he was sure, be capable of cutting quite a decent figure in society. What a pity it was! Where had she picked up the distressing opinions that forced her to make such a melancholy spectacle of herself?

He felt that he must at any rate let her know that he had seen her; and using the juice of a flower stem as ink he wrote the following poem on a piece of thickly folded paper: 'Forgive me that at your wicker gate so long I stand. But from the caterpillar's bushy brows I cannot take my eyes.' He tapped with his fan, and at once one of the little boys ran out to ask what he wanted. 'Take this to your mistress,' he said. But it was intercepted by the maid, to whom the little boy explained that the poem came from the fine gentleman who had been standing about near the gate. 'Woe upon us all,' cried the maid, 'this is the handwriting of Captain So-and-So, that is in the Horse Guard. And to think that he has been watching you mess about with your nauseous worms!' And she went on for some time lamenting over the girl's deplorable oddity. At last the insect-lover could bear it no longer and said, 'If you looked a little more below the surface of things you would not mind so much what other people thought about you. The world in which we live has no reality, it is a mirage, a dream. Suppose someone is offended by what we do or, for the matter of that, is pleased by it, does his opinion make any difference to us in the end? Before long both he and we shall no longer even appear to exist.'

Several of the younger servants had by now gathered round. They found her argument hard to answer, but secretly felt that this was a very dismal view of life. It was not thought likely that she would send an answer, but the Captain was still waiting at the gate and the little boys, who had now all been called back into the house, said the gentleman was looking very unhappy; upon which everyone urged her to write something, and very reluctantly she sent the poem, 'By this you may know the strangeness of my mood. Had you not called me *kawamushi*,[6] I would not have replied.' To which he answered, 'In all the world, I fear, exists no man so delicate that to the hairtips of a caterpillar's brow he could attune his life.' Then he went back laughing to his home.

What happened next will be found in the second chapter![7]

from Tsutsumi Chūnagon Monogatari

---

[6] Hairy caterpillar.
[7] No second chapter exists.

Comradely Love
A Sight in Camp in the Daybreak Grey and Dim

Walt Whitman

A sight in camp in the daybreak grey and dim,
As from my tent I emerge so early sleepless,
As slow I walk in the cool fresh air the path near by the hospital tent,
Three forms I see on stretchers lying, brought out there untended lying,
Over each the blanket spread, ample brownish woollen blanket,
Grey and heavy blanket, folding, covering all.

Curious I halt and silent stand,
Then with light fingers I from the face of the nearest the first just lift the blanket;
Who are you elderly man so gaunt and grim, with well-grey'd hair, and flesh all sunken about the eyes?
Who are you my dear comrade?

Then to the second I step – and who are you my child and darling?
Who are you sweet boy with cheeks yet blooming?

Then to the third – a face nor child nor old, very calm, as of beautiful yellow-white ivory;
Young man I think I know you – I think this face is the face of the Christ himself,
Dead and divine and brother of all, and here again he lies.

Greater Love

Wilfred Owen

Red lips are not so red
   As the stained stones kissed by the English dead.
Kindness of wooed and wooer
Seems shame to their love pure.
O Love, your eyes lose lure
   When I behold eyes blinded in my stead!

Your slender attitude
   Trembles not exquisite like limbs knife-skewed,
Rolling and rolling there
Where God seems not to care;
Till the fierce love they bear
   Cramps them in death's extreme decrepitude.

Your voice sings not so soft, –
   Though even as wind murmuring through raftered loft, –
Your dear voice is not dear,
Gentle, and evening clear,
As theirs whom none now hear,
   Now earth has stopped their piteous mouths that coughed.

Heart, you were never hot
   Nor large, nor full like hearts made great with shot;
And though your hand be pale,
Paler are all which trail
Your cross through flame and hail:
   Weep, you may weep, for you may touch them not.

On Jane Austen's Death

Letter from Cassandra Austen to Fanny Knight

Winchester Sunday

My dearest Fanny – doubly dear to me now for her dear sake whom we have lost.

She did love you most sincerely, & never shall I forget the proofs of love you gave her during her illness in writing those kind, amusing letters at a time when I know your feelings would have dictated so different a style. Take the only reward I can give you in my assurance that your benevolent purpose *was* answer'd; you *did* contribute to her enjoyment. Even your last letter afforded pleasure, I merely cut the seal & gave it to her; she opened it & read it herself, afterwards she gave it me to read, & then talked to me a little & not unchearfully of its contents, but there was then a languor about her which prevented her taking the same interest in any thing, she had been used to do.

Since Tuesday evening, when her complaint returnd, there was a visible change, she slept more & much more comfortably, indeed during the last eight & forty hours she was more asleep than awake. Her looks altered & she fell away, but I perceived no material diminution of strength & tho' I was then hopeless of a recovery I had no suspicion how rapidly my loss was approaching. – I *have* lost a treasure, such a Sister, such a friend as never can have been surpassed, – she was the sun of my life, the gilder of every pleasure, the soother of every sorrow, I had not a thought concealed from her, & it is as if I had lost a part of myself. I loved her only too well, not better than she deserved, but I am conscious that my affection for her made me sometimes unjust to & negligent of others, & I can acknowledge, more than as a general principle, the justice of the hand which has struck this blow. You know me too well to be at all afraid that I should

On Jane Austen's Death

suffer materially from my feelings, I am perfectly conscious of the extent of my irreparable loss, but I am not at all overpowerd & very little indisposed, nothing but what a short time, with rest & change of air will remove. I thank God that I was enabled to attend her to the last & amongst my many causes of self-reproach I have not to add any wilfull neglect of her comfort. She felt herself to be dying about half an hour before she became tranquil and aparently unconscious. During that half hour was her struggle, poor soul! she said she could not tell us what she sufferd, tho she complain'd of little fixed pain. When I asked her if there was any thing she wanted, her answer was she wanted nothing but death & some of her words were 'God grant me patience, Pray for me oh Pray for me'. Her voice was affected but as long as she spoke she was intelligible. I hope I do not break your heart my dearest Fanny by these particulars, I mean to afford you gratification whilst I am relieving my own feelings. I could not write so to any body else, indeed you are the only person I have written to at all excepting your Grandmama, it was to her not your Uncle Charles I wrote on Friday. – Immediately after dinner on Thursday I went into the Town to do an errand which your dear Aunt was anxious about. I returnd about a quarter before six & found her recovering from faintness & oppression, she got so well as to be able to give me a minute account of her seisure & when the clock struck 6 she was talking quietly to me. I cannot say how soon afterwards she was seized again with the same faintness, which was followed by the sufferings she could not describe, but Mr Lyford had been sent for, had applied something to give her ease & she was in a state of quiet insensibility by seven oclock at the latest. From that time till half past four, when she ceased to breathe, she scarcely moved a limb, so that we have every reason to think, with gratitude to the Almighty, that her sufferings were over. A slight motion of the head with every breath remaind till almost the last. I sat close to her with a pillow in my lap to assist in supporting her head, which was almost off the bed, for six hours, – fatigue made me then resign my place to Mrs J. A. for two hours & a half when I took it again & in about one hour more she breathed her last. I was able to close her eyes myself & it was a great gratification to me to render her these last services. There was nothing convulsed or which gave the idea of pain in her look, on the contrary, but for the continual motion of the head, she gave me the idea of a beautiful statue, & even now in her coffin, there is such a sweet serene air over her countenance as is quite pleasant to contemplate. This day my dearest Fanny you have had the melancholly intelligence & I know you suffer severely, but I likewise know that you will apply to the fountain-head for consolation & that our merciful God is never deaf to such prayers as you will offer.

The last sad ceremony is to take place on Thursday morning, her dear remains are to be deposited in the cathedral – it is a satisfaction to me to think that they are to lie in a Building she admird so much – her precious soul I presume to hope reposes in a far superior Mansion. May mine one day be reunited to it. – Your dear Papa, your Uncles Henry & Frank & Edwd Austen instead of his Father will attend, I hope they will none of them suffer lastingly from their pious exertions. – The ceremony must be over before ten o'clock as the cathedral service begins at that hour, so that we shall be at home early in the day, for there will be nothing to keep us here afterwards. – Your Uncle James came to us yesterday & is gone home to day – Uncle H. goes to Chawton to-morrow morning, he has given every necessary direction here & I think his company there will do good. He returns to us again on Tuesday evening. I did not think to have written a long letter when I began, but I have found the employment draw me on & I hope I shall have been giving you more pleasure than pain.

Remember me kindly to Mrs J. Bridges (I am so glad she is with you now) & give my best love to Lizzy & all the others. I am my dearest Fanny

> Most affect^{ly} yrs
> CASS. ELIZTH AUSTEN

I have said nothing about those at Chawton because I am sure you hear from your Papa.

The Girl in the Pink Hat

Charlotte Perkins Gilman

My sister Polly and I had a 'stateroom', but we did not sit in it all the time. The car was not at all full, and I like to move about and look at the scenery from all sides.

Polly is a dear girl, but her best friends admit she is a trifle odd in appearance. She will wear her red hair pulled down over her ears and forehead and neck – that's a switch, too; with a squushy hat drooping over the whole; and big yellow-glassed shell goggles and a veil besides. Also one of those long travelling cloaks, sort of black silk duster. I never could see how people can stand veils over their eyes, and mouths, and noses – especially noses; they tickle so.

But I'm very fond of Polly, and she is really a good-looking girl, when properly dressed. She's a romantic soul, and good as gold. I am romantic, too – but not good.

We were coming home from a long trip, away out to the Coast and back, and the home stretch was tiresome. Somewhere about Schenectady it was. Polly was reading another of her interminable magazines, and I was prowling about after variety and amusement.

There was a day-coach just ahead, and I slipped in there for a change, and found an empty seat.

Just in front sat a young couple, with their heads pretty close together, and I watched them idly, for she was a pretty, eager-looking girl in a soft pink hat, and he quite an impressive fellow – rather too much so, I thought.

Presently I caught a note of trouble in her voice, and a low insistence in his – low, but quite audible to me. The seat in front of them was empty, and I dare say he thought the one behind was too; at any rate they talked, and I couldn't help hearing them.

The amazing way in which people bare their hearts to one another, in streetcars or steam cars, or in steamer chairs, has always been a wonder to me. You cannot accuse the travelling public of eavesdropping when it hears the immediate fellow sufferers in the New York subway explaining their economic disabilities or their neighbours in the day-coach exhibiting a painful degree of marital infelicity.

In my own travels I become an unwilling mother confessor to all about me, for my ears are unusually keen, and seem especially so on the cars. Perhaps it is because the speakers, to overcome the noise of the wheels, raise their voices or sharpen them to a peculiarly penetrating pitch. At any rate I can hear them, right and left, front and rear, which is sometimes interesting, sometimes tedious, sometimes acutely disagreeable.

This time it was interesting, very.

'I tell you it is not my fault,' he was saying, in a low restrained voice, but as one whose patience was wearing thin. 'I couldn't help it if the car was stalled, could I? And then we *had* to catch this train. I have an engagement in the city I can't afford to miss.'

'You can't attend to it tonight, can you?' she asked, evidently trying to keep control of herself, not to be frightened, and not to lose faith in him. Yet a note of suspicion would struggle through in spite of her.

'Why can't we stop off at Albany and—' she spoke low, but I heard it, the little hesitant girlish voice, with a touch of awe at the words '—be married, and then take a later train to New York?'

'What *is* the difference, my dear,' he protested, 'whether we're married in Albany or in New York?'

'What time do we get to New York?' she asked.

'About nine,' he said, and then I became really alert, for I knew it would be about eleven.

'And you can arrange for it then – tonight?' she persisted. 'Isn't your licence for Ohio?'

'What a careful soul you are, my dear,' he replied airily. 'Yes, that licence was for Ohio, of course, and I could hardly get one in New York tonight. But there are more ways than one of being married in New York, you will find. People can be married, legally and properly married, before a notary public, and I have a

The Girl in the Pink Hat

friend who is one. Nothing could be simpler. We call him up, take a taxi to his apartment, make our deposition and have it all properly set down with a big red seal – tonight. Then if you want to go to The Little Church Around the Corner tomorrow and have it 'solemnized,' you may.'

He talked too much. Also, though I sat behind, I could 'smell his breath.' And I saw that the girl was not satisfied. Evidently she was not as green as he had thought her. Either from romances or at 'the movies' she had known things of this sort to be done – with sad results.

It must be a terrible thing in the mind of an affectionate young girl to have to distrust her lover. I judged, from what I had gathered, that she had planned a perfectly good marriage, in her home state, before starting on this journey; that some trifle about that incident of the stalled car had upset her, started her to thinking, and that his drinking, on their wedding trip, seemed a suspicious circumstance to her.

She was visibly alarmed, yet striving still to keep her trust, not to accept the horrible alternative which forced itself upon her mind. She sat still for a minute or two, looking out of the window, while he fondled her in a vain attempt to substitute caresses she did not want for the reassurance he could not give.

She made up her mind presently.

It was a very firm little chin I now observed, as she turned squarely toward him, a face pale but quite determined. She smiled too, trying hard to hold her illusions.

'A bride has *some* privileges, surely,' she suggested with an effect of buoyancy, 'even an eloping bride. I prefer to be married in Albany, if you please, my dear.'

It was a pity for this gentleman's purposes that he had taken that drink, or those drinks. It was a little too much, or not quite enough. It made him irritable.

'But I don't please,' he said testily. 'I did all I could to please you – fixed up to have it all done in Elyria this morning. But we slipped up on that – and now I don't propose to stop over in Albany. It's all nonsense, Jess – only means delay and trouble – I don't know anybody in Albany, and I know plenty in New York.

119

And I tell you I've got to be there in the morning, and I will. And you'll be Mrs Marsh before midnight, all right, all right —'

'I know somebody in Albany,' she answered. 'I have an old friend there; she was my Sunday school teacher. I can stay there over night, or for some days, and you can come up with another licence and marry me.'

Even then, if he had been quite sober he could have satisfied her. She was fairly trembling at her own daring, and quite ready to break down and cry on his shoulder and own she was a goose – if he said the right thing.

But he did not. He tried to assert a premature authority.

'You'll do nothing of the sort,' he told her sharply. 'You're my wife, or will be in a few hours, and you're going with me to New York.'

She lifted her head at that.

'I'm going to get off at Albany,' she answered.

'You haven't so much as a nickel, my dear,' he said disagreeably, 'to 'phone with even, or take a car.'

'I'll walk!' she said.

'You haven't your bag either,' he told her. 'It's in the baggage car and I've got the checks.'

'I don't care – Miss Pierce will take care of me.'

'And suppose Miss Pierce happens not to be there,' he suggested. 'A nice pickle you'd be in – in Albany – at night – alone – no money and no bag – eh, my dear!'

He put his arm about her and hugged her close. She permitted it, but returned to her plea.

'Julius! You'll stop if I want to, surely! Or if you can't, you'll let me. Just get my bag for me, and give me a dollar or two – you're not going to try to *make* me go to New York – against my will?'

'I'm tired of this,' he replied, with sudden irritability. 'Of course you are coming to New York. Now just make up your mind to it.'

'Julius – I'm sorry to – to – set myself against you so, but I have made up my mind. I mean to get off at Albany. If you won't get my bag, I shall appeal to the conductor —'

The Girl in the Pink Hat

He sat up at that, squared his shoulders, and laid an arm across the back of the seat, bending towards her, and speaking low. But I could still hear.

'We've had all we're going to of this – do you hear? You don't know it, but I'm what they call a "plainclothesman". Do you see that star?' From his gesture, and the direction of her frightened eyes, her little gasp, I felt as if I saw it too. 'Now, you sit tight and make no more fuss till we get to the city,' he muttered. 'If you appeal to the conductor – or anybody else, I'll simply tell 'em that you're a well-known criminal I'm taking back. And if you raise any rough stuff I've got the bracelets – see?'

She saw. I heard them chink in his pocket.

'Shall I put them on, or will you be quiet?' he asked, and she sank down defeated.

'Now a fellow can get a little peace, I guess?' said Mr Marsh, and leaned his head back on the red plush.

He kept stern watch of her as we drew toward Albany. I knew he would, and I slipped silently out to consult with Polly. She was immensely excited, and full of plans for a dramatic rescue, but I persuaded her it was not safe.

'He's got the star and the handcuffs,' I told her. 'The girl has nothing but her word – we couldn't do it – not and be sure of it. And besides, it would make a terrible scene – she'd never get over the publicity. Wait now – I see how we can work it. Would you be willing to get off at Poughkeepsie – take a later train or stop over night, as you like?'

'What for?' demanded Polly. 'Of course I'm willing – but how does it help her?'

'Why, he'll be watching so that she can't get off – but he wouldn't stop you. Here – give me that writing tablet, please. I'll tell you directly – but I want to get this done before we're in – or I'll lose that seat. I'll come back as quick as I can and tell you – I'm sure we can do it.'

So I took paper and pencils, and slipped softly back into the seat behind them.

After we left Albany his vigilance relaxed, and presently he was dozing beside her, a sufficient obstacle to her exit.

I swiftly wrote a careful explanation of my overhearing them, of my appreciation of her difficult position, and of her inevitable wish to avoid a noisy scene. Then I proposed my plan – simple enough and calling only for a little courage and firmness on her part – and slipped it in near the window; he couldn't see it – even if awake.

'Have you a watch?' I wrote. 'If you have, look at it now, please.' And I had the pleasure of seeing her do so.

'We get to Poughkeepsie at nine.' I wrote. 'At about fifteen minutes before then, say that you must go the dressing room – he can't refuse that privilege. Go in there first, and shut the door. Take your hat off, and hide it under your dress. I shall be down near there, and when I open the door, you crouch down and slip through into the next car, into the stateroom – this end close to the door, you know. You'll see my sister there – red hair, yellow glasses. She'll tell you what to do. You can look around and see if you think I'm trustworthy. If you think so, you can nod.'

She looked presently, and I'm sure my good-natured, strong-lined, spinsterish face seemed reliable. So she nodded, with determination.

Then I went back to Polly and explained all that I had in mind, the two of us engaging in eager preparations. As the time approached, I entered the day-coach once more, taking the little shut-in seat just opposite the woman's retiring-room, and was all eyes and ears for my plan's fulfillment.

Sure enough, I saw her coming down the aisle, holding the seat backs as the car swung forward. He was watching her too, saw her safely inside with the door shut, and seemed satisfied. He knew she could not get off the train going at that rate.

Then I rose, as if to enter the little place myself, and unlatched the door. Finding it occupied, I came forward a little and stood by the water-cooler, my coat on my arm filling as much of the aisle as possible. She slipped out like a sly child, and I presently followed, stopping to try to enter the dressing-room in vain; opening and closing the rear door with easy indifference.

Before we ran into Poughkeepsie, he must have become anxious, for he started to search the train.

Ours was the next car, our stateroom the first place to look, and he looked accordingly. He saw only a lady with low-curved red hair, a squushy hat, yellow glasses, a veil, a long duster coat, reading a magazine, and my spinsterish self, knitting for the soldiers.

I watched him go down the aisle, questioning a lady near the door – had she seen a girl in a pink hat go through the car? She had not, and resented being asked.

He rushed into the next one, soon came back, again questioning and searching – and as the train stopped, leaped to the platform. Small chance would any pink-hatted, light-coated girl have had of escape on that platform. Only a few got off and he watched every one of them. But naturally he would not know my sister in a neat travelling hat and waterproof coat. How should he?

And as naturally, he would not know my sister, or what certainly appeared to be my sister, wearing that long red switch of which my sister was so proud, her squushy hat, her long duster, her yellow glasses, and her veil. She sat reading as before, and when our friend came through the train again, this time accompanied by the conductor, she barely looked up from her page.

'You need not intrude upon these ladies,' said the conductor, glancing at us. 'I recognize them both.'

'She may have hidden herself in their dressing-room,' the man insisted. But that was easily shown to be empty, and he backed out, muttering apologies.

'Steady, my dear, steady,' I urged, as I saw her trembling with the excitement of that search. 'That's the last of it, I'm sure. He'll go all over the train – and then he'll think he must have missed you at Poughkeepsie.'

We had closed our door by this time, and she could breathe in peace, and speak even, though she would not raise her voice above a whisper.

'He'll be waiting when we get off – he'll be sure to know me then. I'm so afraid!' she said.

'You haven't a thing to be afraid of, my dear child,' I told her. 'My car will be there. You shall come home with me for tonight, and tomorrow we'll talk of the future plans. Or – if you prefer – we'll buy a return ticket to Elyria, and you shall be home again tomorrow.'

'I can't think' she said. 'I'm so frightened. It has been – just awful! You see, I – I *loved* him! I was going to *marry* him – and to have all that turned into – into this!'

'See here, child, you mustn't talk about it now. You've got to keep a straight face and be Sister Polly till we're out of the woods. Just read one of those foolish stories – it'll take up your mind.'

And happening on one of Leroy Scott's doubly involved detective stories, she actually did forget her own distresses for a while following those of other people.

As we proceeded in a dignified manner up the long platform, attended by two red-capped porters, her hand upon my arm, I felt her start slightly.

'There he is,' she said. 'He's just inside the gate. But how funny! He's got another hat – and another coat – how funny! But I'd know his moustache anywhere.'

It was funny, even funnier than she thought. Sister Polly in Poughkeepsie had not been idle, and my young brother, Hugh, had received a telegram as long as a letter and marked 'Rush!' He was on hand, standing near the gate, and looking sharply about him and behind him were two other men who also seemed interested in the crowd.

As we came through, the sharp eyes of Mr Marsh caught the look of terror in the face beside me, and recognizing it in spite of all Polly's wrappings. He started towards her, and she shrank against me with a pitiful little cry, but Mr Marsh was checked in his career by a strong hand on either arm.

'That's him, and he's wanted all right,' said one of his captors, while the other, not too gently, removed his moustache.

Then my young brother, Hugh, with a quizzical smile, took the handcuffs out of that threatening pocket, and they were slipped in place by experienced hands.

'You've certainly had one narrow escape, child,' said Hugh to our young guest.

Tich Miller

Wendy Cope

Tich Miller wore glasses
with elastoplast-pink frames
and had one foot three sizes larger than the other.

When they picked teams for outdoor games
she and I were always the last two
left standing by the wire-mesh fence.

We avoided one another's eyes,
stooping, perhaps, to retie a shoelace,
or affecting interest in the flight

or some fortunate bird, and pretended
not to hear the urgent conference:
'Have Tubby!' 'No, no, have Tich!'

Usually they chose me, the lesser dud,
and she lolloped, unselected,
to the back of the other team.

At eleven we went to different schools.
In time I learned to get my own back,
sneering at hockey-players who couldn't spell.

Tich died when she was twelve.

Daphne Morse

Pamela Gillilan

I'd not thought of her for twenty years
except from time to time, coming across
the old snap of us at Scarborough,
its yellowed monochrome
showing us both laughing on the beach,
my springing red hair printed as dark
as her lustrous black.

Daphne Morse. We were always laughing together,
seeing facades as faces, windows as eyes,
sharing jokes and confidences.
And how we admired each other! And sought
adventure, making aimless journeys,
lodging in attics and cottages, discovering
high moors in the short summer.

It was so long ago, her death,
the scar of it healed, faded;
and yet today unreasonably, unprompted,
I've grieved with a clear bitterness
for her, shortlived
and lovely Daphne Morse.
Thought how her cheeks bloomed
and her throat was smooth
and so were mine, bloomy, smooth.

The looking-glass
is half my present grief.

Activities

Romantic Love

Background notes

Elizabeth Smart and Grace Nichols, from Canada and Guyana respectively, both chose to live in England as adults, earning a living from journalism as well as novels and poetry. Philip Larkin was the Poet Laureate until his death in 1985; he was a prolific and widely esteemed poet whose work treated all aspects of human relationships. Kate Chopin (1850–1904) was a remarkable writer from the American South, she specialized in stories about Louisiana where the French as well as the British influence had been strong. *The Song of Solomon*, also called the Song of Songs, is one of the most famous and most poetic sections of the Old Testament. Its origins are rather obscure but it is attributed to King Solomon himself, one of the most important Kings of Israel. It is traditionally viewed as a metaphor for spiritual love, but modern interpreters of the Bible suggest that it is in fact a collection of poems by several poets. Ernest Hemingway (1899–1961) was also influenced by other cultures in his writing but was always intent on the achievement of an American idiom in his work.

Love (Grace Nichols)

Pair work

The poet uses several images about what love is and what love 'is not', what does each of these images add to the poem?

Love (Philip Larkin)

Pair work

1 Is this a love poem?
2 Read this poem and Grace Nichols' aloud and try to agree on how they should be read for maximum effect. Can such contrasting poems both be true about love?

Group work

Both poems are called *Love* but they are very different. Discuss together a subtitle for each one that would help to provide a first time reader with a clue to each poem's meaning.

Activities

Written assignment

Write a commentary on the poems explaining your reactions to each one. You might consider for each poem the choice of words and images, the use of lines and verses, the moods and emotions expressed. Try and explain why they sound so different and why they leave the reader with such contrasting feelings.

Love (from *An Introduction to Psychology*)

Pair work

1 Should marriage always be based on love?
2 If older people, such as parents, were against the partner of your choice do you think you would listen to their advice? Do they have the right to give advice when you are over sixteen? (This is the legal age for marriage with a parent's consent, at eighteen you no longer need anyone's consent.)?

Group work

Look closely together at the section on romantic love beginning 'The concept of romantic love ...'. What are the group's views about marriage and love? Do you all agree with the survey? Finally do you believe that 'if romantic love disappears from the relationship that is sufficient reason to end it.'

Written assignments

1 This extract about love is taken from a text book and uses very cautious and formal language. Choose an aspect of love, or more than one, from the following list, and write your own text book piece or pieces. Choose from: jealousy, rivalry, love at first sight, opposites attract, being jilted, 'two-timing'. You may think of many more.
2 The writers say that long lasting relationships have more to do with hard work and equality than anything else. Work out a 'Guide to Good Relationships' which explains how couples can make their partnerships last.

Love on the Bon-Dieu

Pair work

Imagine that you are both Azenor's friends. Discuss together if you would advise him to marry such a poor girl.

Activities

Group work
Read over the background notes about Kate Chopin and then look closely at the conversations in the story. Make some notes on the way French language and English language are mixed together. Try reading some of the conversations out loud.

Written assignments
1 Write a continuation of the story in which Azenor tries to explain to Père Antoine what his plans are. You could also describe some reactions from other local people including Madame Zidore.
2 Write an extract from a travel guide describing the atmosphere, landscape and language of the countryside around the Bon-Dieu.

By Grand Central Station

Group work
In this section the writer tries to capture and express the feeling of being totally in love and to do this she chooses her individual words and sentences with great care. Working together try and explain how she uses language to convey this sense of rapturous love. You might begin by looking over the text and picking out words or phrases that seem especially effective in creating the feeling of overwhelming love.

Written assignments
1 Take a section that you especially like from this extract and rearrange its phrases into the shape of a poem. Write a commentary explaining why you chose that section and why it makes a good poem.
2 Take any emotion, e.g. love, anger, fear, and write a piece that really brings out the emotion through the language you use. It may help you to think of a situation that would provoke this particular emotion to give your writing a context.

The Song of Solomon

Pair work
If the Background Notes did not tell you where this piece came from would you still know it was from the Bible? Is there any evidence in the language to show that it is from the Bible?

Group work
Compare *By Grand Central Station* and *The Song of Solomon*. Look closely at the subject matter and language of each and make notes on:
☐ any similarities of language

Activities

☐ what you feel the writers were trying to achieve
☐ how you can tell that one text is thousands of years old and that the other was written this century
Prepare to report your findings to the rest of the class.

Written assignments
1 Write a continuation of the song, imitating the language and style as closely as you can.
2 Try writing out a section of the song in modern English and then add your comments on what is lost and what is gained in this new version.

Right from the Heart

Pair work
Select three phrases from the article that you feel must come from some time in the past, and make notes of your reasons. Choose three phrases that you feel must be very modern. Give your reasons. Compare your choices with another pair, then select the best three in each category. The whole class can now discuss examples of these chosen phrases to see whether there is general agreement on when they were fashionable.

Group work
Work through the article together and jot down the phrases that you feel come from songs. Then add any similar phrases from songs that are currently in the charts. How can we explain the fact that so many popular songs are about love?

Written assignment
Interview one or two people who are considerably older than you and question them about when they were young. See if they can add to the list of phrases and words in the article. What love songs do they remember from their youth? You could then write this up as a description of how this type of language changes over time.

The End of Something

Pair work
What exactly is it the 'End of'? What relationships exist between the three characters, Nick, Marjorie, and Bill?
   Do you feel sorry for either Nick or Marjorie at the end of the story?

Activities

Group work
Reread the opening section of the story which describes the town as it used to be and, in particular, the mill. Decide as a group whether the story would lose anything if this section was removed.

Written assignment
1 Write a scene for the story which would have come before the part we read. You could write about one of Nick and Marjorie's previous visits to the scene or the conversation between Nick and Bill when Nick explains how he plans to end his relationship with Marjorie. Your scene would take the form of a film or television script or it could be a play scene with stage directions.
2 Write your own story about the end of a relationship. You could follow Hemingway's example and write a good deal of the story through conversation.

Jealous Love

Background notes

Edith Wharton was an American writer who lived most of her life in Europe. She was very prolific despite a late start to her writing career, and wrote a significant number of novels, short stories, travel books and essays. This version of *Roman Fever* is a radio play script by Janet Goodwyn based on an original story by Edith Wharton. Elizabeth Bowen was born in 1899 and grew up with the Twentieth century. She was Anglo-Irish and is best known for her novels, especially those set during the Second World War, for example *The Heat of the Day*. Craig Raine is a well known contemporary poet whose work is especially admired for the way it can startle and surprise the reader. John Donne, (1572–1631) is one of a number of writers known as the metaphysical poets because of the ingenuity of their imagery, often linking subjects like the relationship between married lovers to a solid object like a pair of compasses.

Roman Fever

Pair work
How important is the last line? See if you can agree on what it reveals about what happened in the past.
   Imagine that the two women meet again the following day, take a character each and improvise their conversation.

Activities

Group work

Discuss together whether you could tell very easily that this is a radio script, what features suggest that this script is meant to be heard but not seen? After this discussion take a section of the text and either prepare a dramatic reading or record it to play to the rest of the class.

Written assignments

1 Write another scene for the play in which the secret of Barbara's parentage is revealed to the two daughters. As this is a radio script, consider how you can help the listeners follow the drama by using sound effects and offering suggestions about the tone of voice to be used.

2 Write two diary entries, one for Mrs Ansley and one for Mrs Slade. Imagine that they write the entries on the night the play ends, as they think back on the events of the night of the visit to the Colosseum 25 years ago and of their married lives.

3 Write about a time set in the future in which Barbara and Jenny exchange letters and in which they remember their parents.

The Demon Lover

Pair work

To carry out this activity you will need to interrupt your reading at three points and jot down a prediction about the story. At each point discuss your ideas with your partner and then record your personal view in note form. The three points at which to stop are

☐ '...on this lay a letter addressed to her.' (page 50)
☐ 'How should I...? After twenty-five years...' (page 51)
☐ 'She leaned forward to scratch at the glass panel that divided the driver's head from her own.' (page 55)

Look back over your predictions in the light of what eventually happens and jot down some comments on what they reveal about your thinking on the story.

Group work

Imagine that a television company has decided to make a television play based on the story. They want to include it in a series about ghostly encounters. At this stage the company simply wants three key images from the story that they can use in publicity. They plan to take a photograph for each image and to provide a caption underneath. The group has to decide on these three key images and on the caption for each.

Activities

Written assignments

1 What actually happened to the soldier in the story? Write about this or describe the events in the story from his point of view.
2 Write a newspaper article to appear in the paper on the next day; use your imagination and tell what happened to Mrs Drover.
3 One of the most effective elements in this story is its atmosphere. The detailed descriptions of the house and of Mrs Drover's past life steadily build up a sense of fear and suspense. Try writing a piece of your own which builds up atmosphere in a similar way.

An Attempt at Jealousy

Pair work

Prepare a reading of the poem, either using both your voices or just one, and read it to another pair. Compare your interpretations.

Group work

What have you learned about the two people in the poem? Who are they, what do they do, what are they like? Do you feel that the writer is fair in the way he describes them? What is the writer himself like?

Written assignments

1 Write a reply to the poem by the poet's ex-lover. This might take the form of a letter or the script of a telephone call between the poet and his former lover. If you feel ambitious you could try writing the reply in the same style as the poem.
2 Jealousy is easy to feel and hard to describe. Write your own piece about jealousy, you might describe it as if it were a creature or produce a story about how jealousy can affect people.

Song: Go, and Catch a Falling Star

Pair work

Have a close look at the chatty, almost modern style of the poem and then try reading it aloud taking alternate lines each and keeping the lively rhythm going. What kind of 'voice' or accent suits the poem?

Group work

Look at the poem together and sum up what the writer is suggesting about women. Do any members of the group agree with the view put forward?

Activities

Written assignments

1 Write your own poem about men or women that tries to match the lively style of *Go, and Catch a Falling Star*. You could simply adapt the existing poem by making it more modern in sound or by replacing some lines with lines of your own.

2 Compare the two poems *An Attempt at Jealousy* and *Go, and Catch a Falling Star*. Either write a comparative piece commenting on what you feel the two writers have tried to achieve in the poems or write a reply to their views about women.

Loving the Family and Other Animals

Background notes

Carson McCullers, an American writer from the Southern States, is most famous for her novels, which include *The Heart is a Lonely Hunter* (1940) and *The Ballad of the Sad Cafe* (1951). Douglas Dunn, Elizabeth Jennings, and Tony Harrison are among the most important of contemporary British poets. *Romeo and Juliet* is one of William Shakespeare's early plays featuring romance and among his best known and most popular plays. Alice Walker's best-selling novel, *The Colour Purple*, tells the story of Celie, a poor, black teenager, growing up in the American South of the early Twentieth century. Doris Lessing is a prolific novel and short story writer well known for her science fiction. Antonia Fraser is famous for her work as an historian as well as a novelist and short story writer. The anonymous Japanese writer of *The Lady Who Loved Insects* lived some time in the Heian period, 794–1185.

A Domestic Dilemma

Pair work

It is clear that Emily has come close to being an alcoholic. Thinking about the whole story do you feel that she is depicted as being to blame for the state she is in?

Imagine that one of you is Martin and the other is the family doctor. Martin has gone to see the doctor to ask for advice about Emily. Role play their conversation.

Group work

We know that Emily dropped her daughter 'about a year ago' and Marianne had struck her head. If this were a family near where you lived and you knew what had happened would you inform the Social Services? As a group weigh up the 'evidence' against Emily and think

Activities

about the consequences of involving Social Services. What might this do to the family?

Written assignments

1 Rewrite a part of the story from Emily's point of view. Think carefully about the different moods she displays during the story before deciding how best to put across her feelings.

2 Take the title of the story as a title for one of your own. Start by thinking through what a dilemma is and then writing about another difficult situation.

3 The story concludes with the phrase 'the immense complexity of love'. Does this story succeed for you in describing this complexity? Think carefully before writing about: the way description is used, the way we are shown Martin's feelings, the presentation of Emily and the children, the way particular lines stand out, in your opinion, as especially important.

Arrangements

Pair work

What has the writer come to arrange and how does he feel about it?

Group work

After reading the poem together and reading it through aloud at least once discuss how much of the poem is simply a description of what happens and how much records the feelings and reactions of the writer. How might producing a performance of the poem bring out the range of description and feeling?

Written assignments

1 Whether you have attended a funeral or not try to write down your feelings about them. You could do this in a number of ways. You might think about the customs and rituals of funerals. Do you feel that they are still important? You might write about an actual funeral you once attended. You could write a story or poem about an imaginary funeral. Finally, what do you think it must be like to deal with death all the time, like the man in the green pullover in the poem. You could write something from his viewpoint.

An Arundel Tomb

Group work

These are three questions to discuss and decide upon after a close reading of the poem. At this stage make a note of any difficult

Activities

vocabulary but do not get bogged down in it. Make sure that someone reads the poem aloud before you answer the questions together.

1 What detail of the two statues seems most important in the poem?
2 How old do you think the statues are, what comments about time do you find in the poem?
3 Which line from the whole poem best sums up what the writer is saying, try and give some supporting reasons for your group's feelings.

Written assignments

'What will survive of us is love'. Try writing a piece about something that shows how love survives either from your own experience or using your imagination. You might write about a statue, a tomb or another object like a wedding ring or another piece of jewellery that symbolizes love. You could describe a painting or a photograph that captures a moment of love in someone's life.

Romeo and Juliet

Pair work

Look at each character, Juliet, Capulet, Lady Capulet and the Nurse and make notes for each on the following: their feelings during the scene, who is on whose side, the way you think each one will speak their lines.

Group work

1 Using the notes from your work in pairs create together as dramatic a reading as possible of this scene and then either perform all, or part of it, for the class or tape it.
2 Discuss what you know about the way marriages were arranged in Shakespeare's time. If you feel uncertain about how marriages were arranged then look for an appropriate book or edition of the play that will provide you with some historical information on this. Once you feel reasonably confident then decide whether Capulet's reaction to Juliet's resistance to his choice is justifiable. After this consider whether the Nurse is offering sensible advice to Juliet.

Written assignments

1 Write a version of this scene, or part of it, in modern English. You might like to invent a modern situation as well. Have a close look at the language that Shakespeare uses and think what our modern equivalents would be for some of the most important words and expressions used by the characters.
2 Imagine that one of the characters meets someone they know well just after this scene, for example Capulet might meet an old friend who

Activities

also has a daughter or the Nurse might meet another servant. Write a dialogue between the two in which they talk about what has just happened. You could write this in modern English or try to imitate Shakespeare's language.

Brothers and Sisters

Pair work

What made Alice Walker's oldest brother so different from the younger four? Neither Alice Walker nor her brother cried at her father's funeral but she says that later she could understand and forgive her father. What helped her to forgive him?

Group work

Go through the essay together and pick out the differences between the way the brothers and the sisters behaved and were treated. Alice Walker wrote this piece about her family as they were forty years ago. Does the group think boys and girls are still treated as distinctly as her brothers were from her? In what ways are there still differences in how boys are allowed to behave compared to girls?

Written assignments

1 Write a conversation or an exchange of letters between Alice Walker and her oldest brother in which they reminisce about events in their family's past.
2 Alice Walker describes herself as a 'student of women's liberation'. Is this piece of writing about women's liberation? Does it make you think about the way men and women treat each other?
3 In some ways the essay is about sex education, a very important topic for young people, parents, teachers, politicians, etc. to consider. What do you think about sex education in schools and the home, do you feel that boys and girls should receive exactly the same information about sexual matters? Write an article for one of the broadsheet newspapers setting out your opinions about how schools should deal with the topic of sex education. It might be helpful to imagine that there was an article in the paper the previous week in which a writer argued that sex education is a dangerous thing and has no place in school; you could then begin by agreeing or disagreeing with this extreme view.

Activities

Father to Son

Pair work

What makes the father feel so angry and upset, does he blame himself or his son for their being so far apart?

Group work

The father says he would have his son be 'prodigal'. This refers to a Bible story. Pool all your knowledge about this story to see if it helps your understanding of the poem. Then look at the text again and try to explain how the word 'prodigal' adds to the poem's meaning.

Long Distance

Pair work

1 Work out a reading of the first half of the poem using your two voices to capture the two voices of father and son.
2 How has Tony Harrison tried to help us hear his father's voice? Look closely at the first sections of the first verse where he represents his father's voice. Rewrite a line or two in Standard English and then explain the difference from Harrison's original.

Group work

Decide whether *Long Distance* is the best title for the poem. What others might have been chosen? Give some reasons for your views and your decision.

Written assignments

1 Write a piece summing up your feelings about both *Long Distance* and *Father to Son*. You might cover some of these points: what each poet is trying to say, whether you find the poems have any similarities, how you would decribe the kind of language used by each poet and how their word choices affect your reactions, whether you think they are interesting to compare or not.
2 One poem is from father to son the other from son to father, use your imagination and your own experience to consider such relationships. You might write a reply poem as if you were the father in *Long Distance* or the young son in *Father to Son*. You could instead try creating a mother to daughter or daughter to mother piece.

Flight

Pair work

Why is the girl crying at the end of the story?

Activities

Group work

1 Work together and investigate the way that the idea of 'flight' is used throughout the story. Look closely at the sections where the old man is looking after his birds and compare these to the way he talks about his youngest granddaughter.

2 Alice is about to leave home at eighteen to get married. Does the group feel that eighteen is old enough to get married?

Written assignments

1 Write the diary entries for Alice and for Lucy for the day of the story. As it is an important day perhaps they might write about the past as well as the day itself.

2 Write about your reactions to the story itself. Some of these points may help to focus your ideas. Does Doris Lessing give us a sense of the feelings of each character? Are your sympathies mainly with the old man or the young girl? Do you find the use of the idea of flight a successful one?

Death of an Old Dog

Pair work

To undertake this activity you will need to pause in your reading when you reach the words 'the intercom clicked off' (page 101) and then discuss together how the story will end. Jot down all that you know about what has happened so far and make some notes about each character. Then write down your predicted ending.

Group work

Discuss together why the father and son take the law into their own hands. Think about the father's motive and what he has learned about his own future. Why is the son so attached to the dog? What made the wife get rid of the dog without asking the other two? Having weighed up all the 'evidence' decide if justice is done in the story.

Written assignments

1 Write a newspaper account of the story including some information about what happens to Toddie.

2 Write a description of a scene in which a psychologist, investigating Paulina's death, interviews Toddie.

The Lady Who Loved Insects

Pair work

What were the various reactions of her family and her neighbours to this girl's love of insects?

Activities

Group work

Working together, have a close look at the language of this text. How can you tell that this passage is an ancient piece of writing and also that it is translated from another language? Make notes about any features of the language that provide evidence about the age and origin of the piece.

Written assignments

1 Write the second, 'missing' chapter of the story.
2 Write your own story about someone's unusual affection for a creature or creatures.

Comradely Love

Background notes

Walt Whitman, (1819–1897), America's first and foremost poet, worked in hospitals in Washington DC, caring for the wounded and dying soldiers of the army of the Northern States during the American Civil War, fought between 1861 and 1865. Wilfred Owen, poet of the trenches of the European war of 1914 to 1918 celebrated friendship between men, comrades at arms, just as Whitman did. Cassandra Austen, sister to the more famous Jane, was her devoted friend as well as her sibling and Charlotte Perkins Gilman, early American economist and advanced feminist thinker advocated the coming together of men and women in a highly developed form of communal living. Wendy Cope is one of the best known contemporary English poets, greatly admired for her comic as well as her serious poetry. Pamela Gillilan is a contemporary English writer, whose work concentrates particularly on memories and friendships.

A Sight in Camp in the Daybreak Grey and Dim

Pair work

Having read the poem together carefully consider what kind of music might go well with it to give it the right atmosphere?

Group work

What does the group make of the last two lines? Is Walt Whitman suggesting that this dead man is really 'the Christ himself'?

Activities

Greater Love

Pair work

Make notes on these questions after first discussing together what you know about conditions for the men who fought in the First World War. Then join up with another pair for the group work.
1 Who do you think Owen is describing in the poem?
2 Pick out three lines that you feel confident and clear about and three others that you would like help with.

Group work

Compare your knowledge about the First World War to begin with and then discuss together your notes from Questions 1 and 2 above.

Written assignments

1 Compare *Greater Love* and *A Sight in Camp in the Daybreak Grey and Dim*. You may find the following points useful. Are there similarities in the subject matter of the poems and the way the two poets feel about their dead comrades? Are both poets trying to affect their readers in the same way? Do you have a preference for the language or atmosphere of either poem?
2 Imagine that you were someone involved in a war who had lost a dear comrade, write a piece that captures your feelings. You might, for example, write a letter to a friend explaining what has happened or a journal entry for the day you heard the news.

On Jane Austen's Death

Pair work

What kind of relationship existed between the letter writer, Cassandra, and her sister, Jane? Look closely at the language of the letter to find out how the sisters felt about each other. Do you think that Cassandra will be able to cope with her grief, what does she say in her letter about how she expects to deal with her feelings?

Group work

Choose a paragraph or two and study the language very closely. How can you establish that this piece of English is at least 175 years old?

Written assignments

1 Imagine that Cassandra records a few thoughts for herself in her diary after writing the letter. Try writing such a diary extract using details and language from the original.

Activities

2 Write all or part of Fanny Knight's reply to Cassandra, think especially about what we have learnt from Cassandra about Fanny's personality and her skilful letter writing.

The Girl in the Pink Hat

Pair work
What do we learn, in the course of the story, about the two sisters who save the girl in the pink hat? Go through the story together jotting down all the details you can find about them that help us to understand their characters. Are there details early in the story that help us to anticipate how it will end?

Group work
Does the group think that the story has a message about the behaviour of men and/or women?

Written assignments
1 Charlotte Perkins Gilman was a writer who tried to show that women could be more than equal to men, she has been considered an early feminist. Would you say that this is a feminist story and, if so, is it a good one?
2 Write a newspaper report about the arrest of Julius explaining about the girl's situation, the clever actions of the two sisters, and the help of their brother, Hugh.

Tich Miller

Pair work
After reading the poem aloud together, jot down what we know about Tich Miller, the poet and their relationship, would you say they were friends?

Group work
Is the effect of the poem to make the reader angry with the school children because Tich and the writer were always picked last?

Activities

Daphne Morse

Pair work
After reading the poem aloud together discuss what the last line adds to the poem.

Group work
Prepare a reading of the two poems, *Tich Miller* and *Daphne Morse* for the rest of the class. Try experimenting with your reading rather than simply reading one poem after the other; you might consider how the two poems could be arranged to make one powerful statement to your audience. You could think about reading parts of the poems alternately or carefully weaving them together as if they were one poem.

Written assignments
1 Fortunately most people do not lose their friends but we all tend to fall out with them and have arguments from time to time. Write a poem or story about friends falling out.
2 What makes a good friend? What would make you remember a friend until you were old? Write a description of a good friend; you could base this on a real person or you might prefer to describe an ideal friend.
3 Imagine that you are putting together some poems for a collection, called 'Childhood', perhaps to raise money for charity. If you only had space for one of these two poems, which one would you select and why? Try to write about both poems in explaining your choice.

Extended Activities

An Anthology

This is an activity that you might undertake on your own or with others in a small group.

This particular collection, called *Love*, presents several aspects of love and provides the reader with a selection of pieces about each aspect, e.g. Romantic Love, Jealousy, and so on. However, there are many other kinds of anthology that you can think about putting together, here are some suggestions.

a) Ask all your classmates and friends from other classes to write pieces about 'Love' and encourage them to write about different kinds of love. Once you have all the material you can sort it out into sections. At this stage you can either type up or word process the collection, design a cover and possibly some illustrations to accompany various pieces.

b) Choose a range of interesting pieces about love from different types of literature and write responses or 'answers' to all of them. You can then create a collection that has original pieces and responses or replies providing various points of view for the reader to consider.

c) Ask a selection of pupils and possibly teachers to write about their ideal partners and their definition of real love. You could encourage them to include examples of what happened when they first fell in love. You can then put together a collection which explores the idea of partners and love and which should make interesting reading for everyone at the school.

Love in the Media

The media provide us with a constant flow of ideas and stories about love in all its shapes and forms. It offers both information and opinions about love and about people's views of love. Here are some suggestions about how you might investigate the presentation of love by the media. You can carry out an investigation on your own or in a small group.

a) Newspapers: buy as many papers as you can for a particular day and cut out all stories that relate to love in any way – you will need to decide how broad a definition of love you want to include! Once you have all the material consider what it suggests about society. For example, what do readers seem to want to know about love? How are stories

Extended Activities

about lovers presented? What views are quoted in the papers, what types of people are interviewed for their opinions? After considering these questions, create an exhibition of your cuttings in which you present your ideas about love in society as represented in the press.

b) *Soap operas*: these attract the highest viewing figures of all regular television programmes, one reason seems to be because they contain a great deal about love and romance. Over a period of a week try to watch a range of 'soaps' and to note down which parts of the story lines concern love relationships. How is love represented in these soap operas and how do these images of love relate to love in the real world? Write up a report about 'Love in the Soaps'.

Love Survey

You will often hear that 'things are not what they used to be' or that 'all change is for the worse'; older people often seem to think that things were once better than they are now. This activity asks you to investigate what people think through questionnaires, interviews and surveys. Such an approach needs to be highly organized and is best undertaken by a team who work well together. Section *a)* lists some suggestions for survey topics, but you can easily think of your own. Section *b)* looks at ways of gathering and making sense of your information.

a) Each of these topics is large and would need breaking down into manageable chunks, so for the first topic we have included some ideas about how to break up the topic.

Topic 1: The importance of friendship

You could design a survey asking people to identify what they value in their friends. The best approach might be to ask several people to jot down their views about friends and then to design a questionnaire once you have thought about the views you have collected. A different approach might be to present people with a series of dilemmas, e.g. if you knew that your friend had taken something from another friend what would you do? This approach asks people to consider how they feel that they should behave towards their friends. Another idea is to ask boys and girls to define what a good friend is and then to analyse these definitions to see if they are the same.

Topic 2: Attitudes to marriage

Topic 3: Are pets more lovable than people?

Topic 4: Is jealous behaviour acceptable?

Topic 5: Are older people more interested in religion than young ones?

Topic 6: Do all readers/viewers enjoy romance?

Extended Activities

Topic 7: Should schools have lessons about love or is this the responsibility of the family?

Topic 8: Patriotism, the love of one's country

b) Some or all of the following techniques might be used in collecting information. People can be interviewed and their answers written down, some people might be recorded on audio or video tape.

Questionnaires can be devised and handed out. (It is usually best if all questions have yes/no type answers or if you can provide statements about which people can indicate how far they agree or disagree with them.)

Information that has been collected can be analysed and presented as a talk, a written report, with or without statistics, or made into a radio- or television-style documentary.

Wider Reading

Anthologies

Bitter-Sweet Dreams, Lenore Goodings ed., Virago Upstarts, 1987.
   A collection of writing by the readers of *Just Seventeen* which includes several sections connected to love and friendship.
In Our Image, Andrew Goodwyn ed., Unwin Hyman (now Harper Collins), 1990.
   A varied collection that explores the attitudes of the two sexes towards a range of issues including love and marriage.
Falling for Love, Sue Sharp ed., Virago Upstarts, 1987.
   A book which examines the feelings of teenage mothers about love and parenthood.

The following poetry anthologies are very common in secondary schools either in the stock of the English Department or in the school library and they all have sections on Love and/or related matters like patriotism, friendship, animals and so on. *Touchstones* ed. M. and P. Benton, *Strictly Private* ed. R. McGough, *Voices* ed. G. Summerfield, *Standpoints* ed. J. Foster.

Plays

The following plays are likely to be available in your school and all of them deal with interesting aspects of love. *An Inspector Calls*, by J. B. Priestley, examines the intense conflicts within a family, *Gregory's Girl*, takes a lighthearted look at boy/girl relationships at school, *A Taste of Honey* by Shelagh Delaney explores the difficulties of a young unmarried mother. Many plays by William Shakespeare are centrally concerned with love; amongst these are *Othello*, which examines the tragic consequences of jealous love, *A Midsummer Night's Dream*, which treats the often comic complications of love and obsession, *Julius Caesar*, which deals with the love of country and of power, *Antony and Cleopatra*, which looks at the conflict between romantic love and duty to one's country, and *A Winter's Tale*, which brings together many of these aspects of love in an extended treatment of passionate love and platonic friendship, family and patriotic sentiment.

Wider Reading

Novels

Pride and Prejudice, Jane Austen
The Heat of the Day, Elizabeth Bowen
Testament of Youth, Vera Brittain
Jane Eyre, Charlotte Bronte
Wuthering Heights, Emily Bronte
The Awakening, Kate Chopin
Great Expectations, Charles Dickens
Rebecca, Daphne Du Maurier
The French Lieutenant's Woman, John Fowles
Tess of the D'Urbervilles, Thomas Hardy
Sons and Lovers, D. H. Lawrence
Gone With The Wind, Margaret Mitchell
The Colour Purple, Alice Walker
Brideshead Revisited, Evelyn Waugh
Ethan Frome, Edith Wharton
Oranges Are Not The Only Fruit, Jeanette Winterson